THE COMPLETE BEGINNER'S GUIDE

TO OUTBOARDING

ALSO BY A. H. DRUMMOND, JR.

THE COMPLETE BEGINNER'S GUIDE TO SAILING

SAILBOARDING: A BEGINNER'S GUIDE
TO BOARDBOAT SAILING

THE COMPLETE
BEGINNER'S GUIDE
to
OUTBOARDING

by
A. H. Drummond, Jr.

DRAWINGS BY LARRY TAYLOR

DOUBLEDAY & COMPANY, INC.
GARDEN CITY, NEW YORK
1974

ISBN: 0-385-06538-8
Library of Congress Catalog Card Number 73–11702
Copyright © 1974 by Doubleday & Company, Inc.

78218
4-74

CONTENTS

THE COMPLETE BEGINNER'S GUIDE
TO OUTBOARDING

1. TYPES OF OUTBOARD CRAFT

To an ever-increasing number of Americans, spring has acquired a new meaning. Instead of early wild flowers, oiling the lawn mower, or spading a garden bed, it means getting the boat ready for the water. In many parts of the country this activity starts up before the last snow has melted. At boatyards people muffled to the ears against the cold can be seen scraping boat bottoms, polishing brass fittings, or applying antifouling paint while sloshing around in a morass of melting snow and mud. In backyards throughout the land the same activity is under way by trailer boatmen. Outboard engines, too, get the spring treatment. For those who store them in the garage or cellar, this means new spark plugs, lubrication, and a tryout in a barrelful of water. Others simply pick up their engines after winter storage and spring make-ready at a local shop or boatyard.

This is spring fitting out. Its object is to get the boat ready for use and into the water as early as possible. Most boatmen, you see, take their boating seriously. They appreciate the freedom, the sense of individuality, and the challenge they face whenever a voyage begins. Be it a trip ashore in a "dink" to pick up groceries, a fishing trip on the Mississippi River, water skiing or skindiving, or a boat camping trip, the thrill of taking on the sea is always present. Moreover, it's a feeling that repeats itself anew each time the boatman goes out.

But words alone cannot fully convey the pleasures of boating. Only experience will do this. Unfortunately, however, one cannot just jump into a power boat and take off. Much must be learned and much must be understood before a boat is taken out. That is the purpose of this book.

As you read on, you will discover many important things about outboard and stern-drive powered boats. You will learn a considerable amount of seamanship, how to care for your outboard engine, and some basic piloting skills. You will learn something about reading the weather, and about how to handle a boat under rough conditions. Very important indeed, considering the speeds now possible in outboard craft and the crowded conditions on many of our waterways, you will learn the rules of the road—the traffic regulations for seagoing craft.

As you are well aware, virtually all exciting and rewarding sports carry with them some danger. Power boating is no exception. The careful and well-trained boatman is probably safer in his boat than he is on the highway in the family car—assuming he knows and obeys the rules, and adds a strong measure of common sense to all of his activities.

On the other hand, the careless and uninformed skipper runs many risks. He may find himself caught in a sudden storm and not know what to do. He may some day face a fire or explosion on his boat, or fall overboard while under way and be left behind. Safety afloat, as you will discover, is an important part of boating. By first learning how to handle a boat under power, and then by observing just a few basic rules when you are on the water, you will make boating a source of lifelong enjoyment.

Men and women well advanced in years still enjoy the pleasures of boating, still thrill to the special magic that seems to take place when skipper and boat are attuned to the natural elements. Read on; the sooner you cast off, the better. *Bon voyage!*

CLASSIFICATION OF MOTORBOATS

What is a motorboat? The legal definition, as given by the Motorboat Act of 1940 and amended by the Federal Boating Act of 1958, is as follows: Any vessel (except tugboats and towboats powered by steam) sixty-five feet or less in length and powered by machinery is a motorboat. Thus virtually all vessels powered by outboard engines or stern-drive units are classified as motorboats.

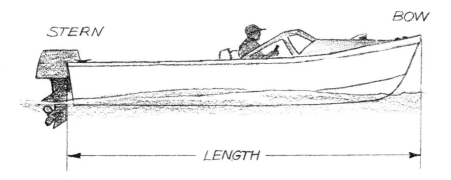

Figure 1. A boat's length is measured from the tip of the bow to the tip of the stern. It does not include projections such as the outboard engine shown here.

The law goes further: It specifies the safety equipment and lights a motorboat must carry and sets up procedures for registering boats and reporting accidents. In addition, most of the states have established regulations that may modify or add to the federal requirements. Do not be discouraged by these federal and state regulations. They have been established for your protection, and work in your favor if you know and obey them. It pays also to be constantly on the defense when on the water. Just as when you are behind the wheel of an automobile, never assume that the other person knows the rules and will obey them. In the vast majority of cases, nothing adverse will ever happen. If you are prepared, however, you may avert the bad accident caused by someone else's careless operation of a boat.

For regulatory purposes, motorboats are broken down into the following four classifications:

CLASS A: Motorboats less than sixteen feet in length.

CLASS 1: Motorboats sixteen feet or more, and less than twenty-six feet in length.

CLASS 2: Motorboats twenty-six feet or more, and less than forty feet in length.

CLASS 3: Motorboats forty feet or more, and less than sixty-five feet in length.

A boat's length, incidentally, is measured end-to-end in a straight line parallel to the surface of the water. Extensions beyond the hull, such as an outboard engine, are not included in this measurement. A boat's length does extend from the tip of the bow, however, and includes the portion of the bow section that overhangs the water.

By far the vast majority of motorboats used for recreational purposes are under twenty-six feet in length. These boats thus fall in classes A and 1. Moreover, most of these boats are powered by one or two outboard engines or by a stern-drive rig. Stern drive, or inboard-outboard (I/O) rigs combine the advantages of an inboard engine with the tilting and detachability features of the drive portion of an outboard engine. For our purposes, it is enough to know that stern-drive boats are steered in the same manner as outboard-powered boats. Steering is accomplished by shifting the direction of the propeller's thrust.

Since the handling characteristics of stern-drive boats are almost identical to those of outboard-powered boats, this book is really about both types of boat. For purposes of simplicity, however, we will refer only to "outboards" from this point on. Just keep in mind as you go along that whatever is said about the handling of an outboard-powered boat applies also to stern-drive boats.

WHY AN OUTBOARD?

A good question. Let's set the stage for an answer that will fill your needs. To begin with, you're reading this book because you are interested in small powerboats. You may, in fact, be reading the book because you have made the decision to buy a boat. Let's assume this is the case, and take a look at the numerous advantages of outboard-powered boats.

Do you plan to trailer your boat? Most outboards are designed to be trailered to the water's edge, where they are relatively easily launched and recovered. For most inboard-powered craft this is impossible. The rudder, propeller and shaft, and skeg project downward from the bottom of the boat, and thus prevent easy launching from a trailer. Clearly, portability is a major advantage of an outboard rig. You take it with you to the water of your choice. Inboards are usually moored in one place, which limits the range for cruising.

Is storage a problem? Inboard boats are usually so heavy they must remain at the boatyard. This means a mooring or berth in the summertime, and yard storage during the winter. Both cost money—lots of it. An outboard, however, can be stored in the location of your choice right on its trailer. For most people this means the backyard.

Aside from convenience and virtually no cost, there is one other distinct advantage to storing your boat in the backyard. When spring fitting-out time rolls around, it is right there, handy to both you and your tools. Don't overlook another potential cost savings. Most marinas and boatyards will permit you to work on your boat when it is stored in the yard, but they usually expect you to purchase all necessary supplies from them. Considerable savings on paint and other materials can be made if you are free to shop around.

Are you concerned about engine maintenance? When faced with an engine problem he can't solve himself, the outboard skipper simply removes the engine from the boat and takes it to the repair shop. Or he trailers the boat and engine to the shop of his choice. The inboard skipper isn't as lucky. When he has problems the mechanic must come to the boat. Indeed, the boat sometimes has to be hauled out, adding even more to the cost of service. Thus it is both easier and less costly to service an outboard engine.

The propeller and shaft on inboard boats are a major source of problems. They are fixed in place and are often damaged by underwater obstacles. The tilt feature of the modern outboard engine, on the other hand, protects its propeller from most damage. When the lower unit of an outboard strikes an underwater obstacle, the engine tilts up and absorbs the impact. Because of this feature, propellers on outboard engines sustain far less damage. Even if the propeller is damaged beyond repair and must be replaced, the outboard skipper is way ahead. He simply tilts the engine up and replaces the faulty propeller. The inboard skipper is not so fortunate. He will probably have to haul his boat out of the water to make the repair. Or become part fish and replace the propeller under water.

Want lots of space in your boat? If so, then an outboard is probably the boat for you. To begin with, the outboard engine is mounted on the transom at the stern of the boat. For an equivalent boat, an inboard engine would project right up into the middle of the boat's cockpit. You've probably seen the boxy engine housings typical of inboard-powered boats.

Now, how about disadvantages? There are some, of course, but they are not serious when the limitations of the outboard rig are fully understood. For example, there is no way to create the luxury of a large yacht on an outboard-powered boat. The two are simply incompatible. If you want that kind of luxury, shop around for that kind of boat.

There are power limitations also to outboard engines. Today, for ex-

Figure 2. A typical round-bottomed dinghy, useful for running errands, going ashore in strange harbors, and ferrying the kids to a good fishing hole. Note the life preservers on the children, a wise move under all conditions when on the water. (*Photo courtesy of Aero-Nautical, Inc.*)

ample, 125 to 140 horsepower is about the maximum available. Moreover, if two 125-horsepower engines are used together, they do not produce a total of 250 horsepower. The actual power output is closer to 200 horsepower. Thus there is an inherent limit to the amount of power that can be obtained with the use of outboard engines. This, in turn, limits the size and weight of the boat if good performance is desired. A 40-foot cruiser powered by a total of 200 horsepower is going to be a pretty disappointing rig to the skipper who expects more.

Outboard hulls are lighter in weight than inboard hulls. In addition, the hull shape used makes the outboard more sensitive to wind action. A breeze that will skitter an idling outboard about on the water, for example, has no effect on the heavier and deeper-riding inboard hull.

These are minor objections, however, which are easily overcome. On balance, its many advantages make the outboard rig the ideal boat for a wide variety of uses. Millions of people seem to agree, as even the most casual observer of our recreational waterways will attest.

Figure 3. A flat-bottomed pram, constructed of synthetic plastic. With the correct engine, these boats are very useful in and around protected harbors. (*Photo courtesy of Kiekhaefer Mercury.*)

TYPES OF OUTBOARDS

Unfortunately, the legal subdivision of motorboats into classes does not lend itself to practical use. Who ever heard a proud owner boast that he had a "souped-up Class 1 motorboat"? More likely he would say "my boat is a 25-foot deep-V glass runabout powered by twin 50s." This is more like it. The language is more descriptive, and in the spirit of power boating a good deal more colorful. Most important, it evokes a pretty good image in the mind of the listener.

Figure 4. A typical aluminum utility outboard. Boats such as this are most often used for fishing. Speeds up to 20 mph are attainable with a 9.5-hp engine. (*Photo courtesy of Evinrude Motors.*)

There are a great many types of boats powered by outboard engines. Almost too many, in fact, to permit a simple but practical classification. Nevertheless, we can identify and illustrate some five distinct types. Then, to avoid omitting some very interesting "mavericks," we will describe a few rather odd craft designed for special purposes.

Dinghy. The dinghy, a small boat often called "dink" and sometimes "pram" (really a short, flat-bottomed rowboat with a blunt bow), is strictly a utility craft. Dinghies range in length from about six to twelve feet, and can be rowed as well as powered by a small outboard engine. The better-quality dinghies are round-bottomed and constructed of Fiberglas or a synthetic plastic. Flat-bottomed prams are usually constructed of marine plywood.

The dink or pram is not sufficiently seaworthy for use on open waters, so it is to be seen mostly in harbors, marinas, or sheltered anchorages. It makes a fine first motorboat for a youngster, and of course is ideal for running errands when the water is too crowded for larger boats to maneuver. A dinghy is an absolute necessity to the owner of a large cruising boat, be it a sailboat or a power cruiser, for it is often the only way to

Figure 5. Utility or runabout? Large for a utility, yet stripped down and specially equipped for offshore fishing, this boat resists simple classification. Clearly, however, it does what it was designed to do for these fishermen. (*Photo courtesy of Aquasport, Inc.*)

Figure 6. This sport runabout is powered by a 4-cylinder 130-hp engine, among the most powerful available. (*Photo courtesy of Marine Products Operations, Chrysler Corporation.*)

Figure 7. When a pretty girl wants an isolated sandspit for a bit of sun-bathing, what better way to get there than on a waterbug such as this one? (*Photo courtesy of Kiekhaefer Mercury.*)

go ashore in a strange harbor. Thus you will see many large powerboats with a dinghy slung from davits at the stern end. Because of space problems, however, this is not always possible on cruising sailboats. These boats tow the dinghy behind as they cruise from port to port.

Utility. Ranging in length from about ten feet up to fifteen or sixteen feet, the utility is a stripped-down, bare-bones boat. It is designed to get you there and back at the most reasonable cost possible. For the most part, utilities are open boats with little or no fancy trim. If you're looking for comfort, this is not the boat for you.

With a suitable outboard engine, the utility is a fast and economical boat. Its uses cover a wide range: running errands, selling the Sunday papers in a crowded anchorage (often seen by cruising skippers), day fishing trips by father and son, amusing and sometimes abortive attempts at water skiing by youngsters, and so on. In addition, most utilities are easily car-topped. Thus they can be taken along on the family camping trip without the added expense of a boat trailer.

Wood, Fiberglas, aluminum, and molded plastic utilities are available. These boats also come in a variety of hull forms, ranging from the traditional flat or round bottom to such esoteric designs as the modified catamaran or trimaran hull. Even a canoe can be classified as a utility outboard—

Figure 8. The new and the old in fishing craft: the modern outboard and the gaff-rigged schooner. Sport fishing boats such as this outboard are becoming increasingly popular. (*Photo courtesy of Kiekhaefer Mercury.*)

Figure 9. A unique recent innovation, the walk-through windshield permits a comfortable cockpit forward of the helm on this runabout. (*Photo courtesy of Marine Products Operations, Chrysler Corporation.*)

that is, if it is constructed with a blunt stern designed to accommodate an outboard engine. The canoeing purist who uses only paddles for propulsion would probably also agree that a canoe with an outboard bracket is a utility—not a canoe.

Runabout. The queen of the outboard fleet, the runabout is so popular that the prospective buyer faces a bewildering array of choices. Runabouts range in length from less than fifteen feet to a bit over twenty feet, and for the most part are constructed of Fiberglas or aluminum. In addition, they are often loaded with extras. But be careful. Anyone considering the

Figure 10. When the wind drops, a small outboard is the ideal power source for many sailboats. Sailboats up to thirty feet or so in length are now designed to accept outboard auxiliary engines. (*Photo courtesy of Kiekhaefer Mercury.*)

purchase of a runabout would do well to look beyond the fancy accessories and trim to the basic seaworthiness of the boat. Many a new owner, dazzled by the appearance of a boat, has found it less than satisfactory where it counts—on the water.

Runabouts are used for virtually every conceivable purpose, the only exceptions being extended cruising and open ocean passages. These boats are too small, too fragile, and inappropriately designed for extended deep-water work on the open ocean. Although not suitably equipped for long-range cruising, they are, on the other hand, often used for weekend overnight trips. This usually means a sleeping bag on an air mattress, and if the boat is not equipped with a canvas top, possible exposure to the elements. For many, it is still worth the potential discomfort to get away for a weekend.

Figure 11. Surprising as it may seem, this inflatable boat plus a 25-hp engine packs enough power for water skiing. (*Photo courtesy of Avon Rubber Co., Ltd.*)

Figure 12. Light in weight, capable of good speed, and easily stored, inflatable boats are becoming increasingly popular. This one obviously makes a good runabout. (*Photo courtesy of Zodiac of North America, Inc.*)

Figure 13. Great for family outings, the pontoon boat gets you there quickly and comfortably. (*Photo courtesy of Johnson Motors.*)

Many runabouts are fitted with a folding canvas top, a handy accessory in the event of a chilling rain. If there is decking forward, there will probably also be some sort of forward compartment, or cuddy, for the storage of loose gear. Beyond these useful additions, you will often find lots of gleaming chrome instrumentation—very expensive, and usually not required for safe and pleasant boating.

Cruiser. The outboard cruiser is a pocket version of its big sister—the inboard-powered cruising yacht. Outboard cruisers generally do not exceed twenty-five feet in length, which means that the accommodations they carry must be squeezed into a rather small amount of space.

There are three essential features to any cruiser: sleeping accommodations, a head, and a galley. Thus this type of boat is designed for living aboard. It may be a crowded and Spartan life, but it is life aboard. It's surprising how many people demand the utmost in luxury at home while settling happily for the most primitive conditions on a boat. There must be something to "the lure of the sea," after all.

Outboard cruisers may be powered by a single engine or by two mounted side by side on the transom. Usually a separate water-tight hull

Figure 14. Designed by Florida bait fisherman Mark Roberts with the help of Barney Walters, this flat-bottomed aluminum boat successfully hauls up to five tons of bait fish over the Keys flats. This is a prime example of the special versatility that can be built into outboard-powered boats. (*Photo courtesy of* Sea Talk.)

section is constructed at the stern of the boat to accommodate the engine or engines and gasoline tanks. The advantage of this arrangement is that any water splashed aboard drains away and not into the cockpit.

Houseboat. Not too many years ago when someone said "houseboat," the image of a floating raft supporting a boxy hut flashed into the mind. This is no longer the case. Today, after several years of design innovation, houseboats offer just about everything a boatman could desire. These new boats are fast, seaworthy, and roomy beyond belief. Their only drawback is aesthetic appearance. Despite great strides forward, they still look somewhat awkward and boxy. No one, however, can fault the interior accommodations. If you are looking for a "floating miniature apartment," this may very well be the boat for you.

Just a few years ago many of the smaller houseboats were powered by twin outboard engines. With more widespread use of stern-drive propulsion, however, this situation has changed. Today most houseboats sport twin stern-drive units, although a few of the smaller boats are still powered by outboards. Two of these boats are shown among the illustrations in this chapter.

Figure 15. All the comforts of home are incorporated into this stern-drive houseboat. These relatively new craft are fast and reasonably seaworthy. (*Photo courtesy of Nauta-Line, Inc.*)

Figure 16. The Hobo is a pocket-sized houseboat. This Canadian import lends itself well to short-range cruising. (*Photo courtesy of Pamco Boat Products, Ltd.*)

Figure 17. Suitable for fishing, family picnics, and even overnight camping, flat-topped boats such as this can be seen in many areas. (*Photo courtesy of Sea and Air Products, Inc.*)

You-name-it. Considering the ease with which an outboard engine can be attached to a boat, it was inevitable that man's inventive genius should come up with a variety of unusual uses. From the far-out bathtub under power sometimes seen in novelty races to specially designed commercial craft, all these boats have one thing in common: They are designed and constructed to serve a special purpose. The boats illustrated in this chapter are but a few of the many types seen on U.S. waters.

Would you have thought, for example, that it is possible to water ski behind a small inflatable boat? That outboard-powered pontoon boats are ideal for family outings? All this, and more, is possible. One of the great attractions of outboarding is the versatility of the approach. You can mount an outboard on almost anything that floats. This would not always be wise or safe, but it does at least show the enormously wide range of interests and needs that can be served by the outboard engine.

2. OUTBOARD HULLS

DESPITE THE APPEAL of the accessories and other gadgets above the waterline on a boat, how it will perform depends in large measure on the shape of its hull. Thus the potential boat buyer would do well to become familiar with the basic hull types and their performance characteristics. It is obviously important also to match the proper engine to the boat. A superbly designed hull, for example, that is either underpowered or overpowered is sure to be a disappointment to its skipper.

BASIC HULL TYPES: DISPLACEMENT AND PLANING

In the broadest possible sense, there are just two basic hull types (exclusive of hydrofoils and catamarans, which will not be discussed here). These are the *displacement* hull and the *planing* hull. Displacement hulls plow through the water, while planing hulls skim along on the surface of the water. As you have no doubt guessed, the planing hull is capable of far greater speeds than the displacement hull. There are other differences that should also be considered, however.

Displacement hulls, whether standing still or underway, displace (push aside) a volume of water whose weight equals the total weight of the boat. This of course includes everything on board the boat—even people. This is the key to how the displacement hull performs. It literally pushes the water aside as it moves, either forward or astern. Hulls that function this way perform best if they are long and narrow with a rounded bot-

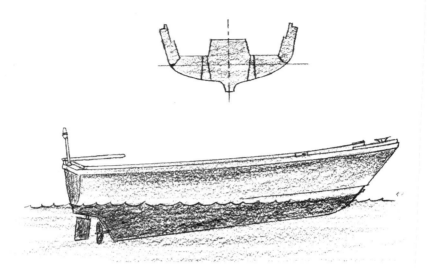

Figure 18. The Bristol Pilot, built by Gull of Bristol, Inc., is a fifteen-foot utility boat with a displacement hull. As the drawing suggests, hulls shaped like this one displace, or push aside, the water as the boat moves forward.

tom. A sharp bow entry and a narrow stern help also. The volume of water pushed aside as the boat moves forward must flow inward and refill the space left by the hull as it passes through the water. In a sense, this space is a cavity in the surface of the water. The displaced water is mounded up around the outer edge of the cavity. The weight of the mounded-up water then pushes it back into the cavity.

The speed of a displacement hull is limited by the shape of the hull and by its waterline length. It turns out that the greater the waterline length, the greater the maximum speed—the *hull speed*—of the boat. Hull speed can be estimated by multiplying the square root of the waterline length by 1.35. For a 25-foot displacement hull of average proportions, for example, the hull speed is about 6.75 miles per hour.

It is possible, although not wise, to drive a displacement hull somewhat beyond its hull speed. When this is done, the boat is moving faster than the displaced water can refill the cavity left by the hull's passing. As a result, the stern of the boat drops into the void, and a strong suction force is produced on the aftersection of the hull. At this difficult angle, applying more power produces more drag and dangerously alters the handling characteristics of the boat. Finally, and not unimportantly, attempting to

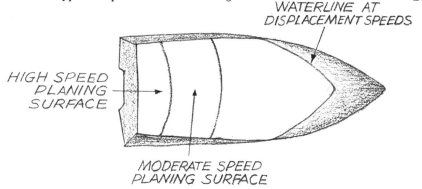

Figure 19. Wetted surface on a planing hull. At planing speeds, lift forces
the hull out of the water so that it skims along the surface.

drive a boat beyond its hull speed is enormously wasteful of fuel. Most
boatmen have better things to spend their money on.

Planing hulls are available in a variety of different shapes. In almost
all cases, however, the stern is broad and the aftersection of the hull's
bottom is flat or nearly flat. This section is the planing surface.

Dead in the water or under way slowly, planing hulls too displace a
volume of water whose weight equals the total weight of the boat. Under
these conditions, the hull is a displacement hull. When speed is increased,
however, water pressure builds up on the broad and flat aftersection of
the bottom. This pressure produces lift. In effect, it pushes the hull out of
the water and on plane. When on plane, the hull skims along the surface
of the water. Moreover, because the hull is skimming along on the surface
and not plowing through the water, there is very little resistance to its
passage.

Speed is the hallmark of the planing hull. This is achieved, however, at
the expense of seaworthiness—the major advantage of the displacement
hull. Planing hulls are indeed fast and maneuverable, but when operated
at high speeds in choppy water their ride can become very hard and uncomfortable. Such boats tend to pound and will often slam viciously into
oncoming waves. This pounding, if allowed to continue, can damage a
hull or perhaps even flip the boat over. As a result, in rough water it is
necessary to reduce speed sharply—often all the way back to displacement speed. Because of this lack of seaworthiness in rough water, boats
with planing hulls should be restricted to relatively smooth waters in
sheltered areas.

Well-designed displacement hulls, on the other hand, knife sharply into oncoming waves instead of pounding. They then lift smoothly and come down more gently as they ride over the seas. In addition, because the bottom of a displacement hull is rounded, such boats roll with less snap and are less likely to flip over.

As pointed out earlier, the aftersection of the bottom of a planing hull is flat or nearly flat. With respect to the forward end, however, there is considerable variety. Forward shapes include the perfectly flat bottom, the V bottom, and the round or arc bottom. With the exception of the perfectly flat bottom, these forward shapes represent an attempt to combine the seaworthiness of displacement hulls with the speed of planing hulls. In the case of the V bottom, for example, the V is deep at the bow but becomes increasingly shallow toward the stern. The idea is to make the bow entry softer and thus reduce pounding in rough water. At the same time, however, the flattened aftersection allows the hull to plane at higher speeds.

Rounding the chines also improves a hull's seaworthiness. This step, however, reduces the hull's maximum speed because the rounded chines effectively reduce the water pressure support on the planing surface. Put another way, the more rounded the chines, the deeper the hull will float in the water. But this increases water drag on the hull, and therefore it decreases the maximum speed attainable.

Theoretically, the ideal planing hull would have a perfectly flat bottom. For such a hull, the more power applied, the faster it would go. Unfortunately, there are disadvantages to this ideal design. Among these are poor entry and very poor handling characteristics at low speeds. *Flat-bottomed* boats thus are fast but dangerous and hard-riding in rough water. A skeg or a fin will provide some directional stability and also reduce skidding in sharp turns. Nevertheless, flat-bottomed boats with hard chines are susceptible to flipping over in high-speed turns.

Shallow *V-bottomed* boats and *arc-bottomed* boats gradually flatten out toward the aftersection of the hull. These hulls are just a bit slower than flat-bottomed hulls, provided they have hard chines. If the chines are rounded, maximum speed drops off significantly. Directional stability and ride are better than in the flat-bottomed hull, however, justifying this design approach.

A fairly recent development is the *deep-V* hull. In this design modification, the V shape runs all the way from the bow to the stern, with little or no flattening toward the aftersection. Such a hull would function as a dis-

Figure 20. As this photo shows, when planing, the after section of the hull skims along the surface of the water. (*Photo courtesy of Aquasport, Inc.*)

placement hull at all speeds if it weren't for a clever design innovation that permits it to plane at higher speeds. The planing surface is provided by building the sides of the V in a series of "steps" running fore and aft, with the bottom surface of each step parallel to the plane of the water. The steps may be constructed by fastening strakes, or moldings, to the bottom of the hull. In the case of Fiberglas hulls they are usually molded in when the hull is laid down.

In use, the stepped deep-V hull is rather unstable at rest and at low speeds. The boat heels more than a flat-bottomed boat, for example. As speed increases, however, lateral stability also increases, and the hull begins to rise as each successive step goes on plane. This progression goes from the outermost pair of steps toward the innermost pair on either side of the keel. Finally, when the hull is on full plane, only a small portion of the V remains in the water. Increased seaworthiness when on plane is the great advantage of this hull type. Instead of slamming into oncoming waves, the deep V slices into them, cushioning the shock. Buoyancy then helps to drive the hull back to maximum plane, and the boat resumes full speed.

Round-bottomed boats are smoother riding than flat-bottomed or V-bottomed craft, but they are slower because the rounded chines reduce the planing support area. Such boats require more power to put them on plane, but they are more stable in high-speed turns. There is also less danger of flipping a round-bottomed boat over.

FORCES ON A PLANING HULL

Displacement hulls plow through the water, pushing it aside as they pass. Planing hulls, on the other hand, skim over the top of the water. But planing hulls at rest and at low speeds perform as displacement hulls. All planing hulls must therefore pass through a transition point—from displacement to planing—when they start at rest and accelerate to planing speeds. This is a rather complicated affair, but it is necessary to understand what happens in order to control the stability of the boat. After all, speeds well in excess of thirty miles per hour are possible when a boat is planing. If the forces controlling stability are not understood by the boat's operator, he will not have adequate control of the boat, and a nasty accident may occur.

The forces acting on a boat at planing speeds are *weight* (the effect of gravitational force), *buoyancy, thrust* (the drive produced by the turning propeller), and *lift* (the upward force exerted on the bottom of the hull by the water as it passes beneath the hull). Now let's examine how these forces come into play as the boat goes from rest to planing speeds. Refer to Figure 23 as you read along.

When the boat is at rest, just two forces—weight and buoyancy—come into play. G in the diagram is the center of gravity of the boat. This is the point somewhere within the boat where all the boat's weight seems to be concentrated. If a cable were attached to this point and the boat lifted free of the water, it would hang on an even keel. B is the center of buoyancy. This is the point at which all of the buoyant force on the boat seems to be concentrated. When a boat is floating freely on an even keel, its weight is exactly counterbalanced by the force of buoyancy. Moreover,

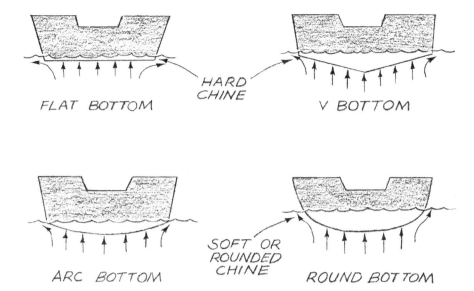

Figure 21. The shapes of flat-, V-, arc-, and round-bottomed boats.

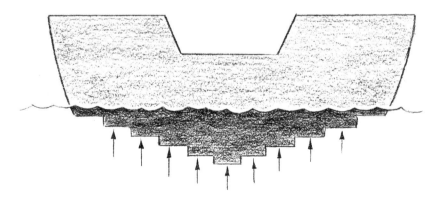

Figure 22. Schematic diagram of the shape of a deep-V hull. The hull is shown at rest in the water. The horizontal "steps" provide the planing surface. The arrows show the direction of lift.

as the diagram shows [Figure 23(A)], the center of gravity G is directly in line vertically with the center of buoyancy B.

Now let's get the boat under way and accelerate to planing speed. At first the boat will move at displacement speeds. Under these conditions, virtually all its support comes from the force of buoyancy. Little or no support comes from either thrust or lift. As a result, the center of gravity G and the center of buoyancy B remain in line with each other.

Just after the boat reaches maximum displacement speed, however, another effect begins to occur. Because of the boat's increased speed, the water passing beneath the hull exerts a greater force on the bottom. This lift force begins to push the bow out of the water. As a result, the wetted surface on the bottom moves aft and thus decreases. But the center of buoyancy B must also move aft in order to remain at the center of the wetted surface. At this point the boat is said to be *surfing;* this occurs midway between plowing and planing.

When a boat is surfing, the forces giving it stability are weight, buoyancy, thrust, and lift. The total downward force is still, of course, weight. The total upward force, however, is no longer supplied by buoyancy alone. This force is now the sum of a decreased buoyant force, a portion of the lift force, and a portion of the thrust. Both lift and thrust are exerted upward on an angle (thrust forward and lift toward the stern). Hence only a portion of each of these forces is exerted straight up. These two, plus the reduced buoyant force, exactly counterbalance the total weight of the boat.

At maximum surfing speed, some of the water bypassing the hull is passing under it, rather than around it as at displacement speeds. This water passing under the hull is the source of lift. But if the lift force were unopposed, it would simply flip the boat bow over stern. This does not happen, of course, because the center of buoyancy has moved aft. This produces a sort of seesaw effect, with the weight of the boat acting through the center of gravity G to force the bow down and the buoyant force acting through the center of buoyancy B to force the stern up [Figure 23 (B)].

As more power is applied and speed further increases, the lift force of the onrushing water progresses toward the stern of the boat and lifts the entire hull higher in the water. Finally, the boat begins to plane as the bulk of the water bypassing the hull is flowing under it rather than around it. At this point, the wake clearly shows that the boat is on plane [Figure 23(C)]. Rather than showing turbulence and producing drag, the wake

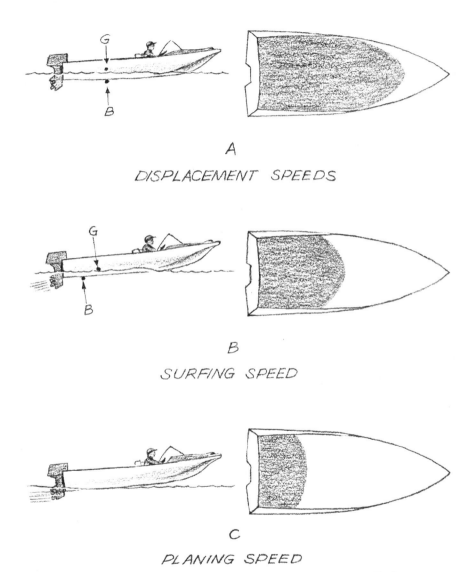

A

DISPLACEMENT SPEEDS

B

SURFING SPEED

C

PLANING SPEED

Figure 23. Attitude of a planing hull and wetted surface at displacement, surfing, and planing speeds. See the text for explanation of the forces acting on the hull at these speeds.

is a smooth and solid platform of water supporting the aftersection of the boat.

The forces acting on the hull are still weight downward and buoyancy, thrust, and lift upward. The upward forces have been redistributed, however, to reflect the change in the boat's performance. Buoyant force, for example, is sharply reduced in favor of lift, which supports almost the entire load. A precise explanation of how these forces act is beyond the scope of this book. Suffice it to say that when at equilibrium on plane the forces are balanced and the boat is stable.

A word or two about planing hull speed seems appropriate. We saw that displacement hull speed is determined by waterline length and hull shape. Planing hull speed, on the other hand, is determined by the surface area of the hull in contact with the water. The smaller this area, in general, the greater the speed attainable. Keep in mind, however, that factors other than the design of the boat affect wetted surface area. The bottom, for example, must be kept clear and free of marine growth, or performance will be decreased. An overloaded boat planes less efficiently because wetted surface area is increased. Some overzealous owners, in fact, have discovered to their chagrin that a more powerful (and heavier) engine can produce poorer results than a lighter engine simply because of the overloading factor.

WOOD, FIBERGLAS, OR ALUMINUM?

Depending on the nature of the average wind and sea conditions under which the boat will be used, the object in buying is to obtain a craft that will be fast, strong, seaworthy, and attractive to the eye. This can be done with any one of the major construction materials—wood, Fiberglas, or aluminum. The choice is up to the buyer. It will help, though, to know something about the structural and performance characteristics of the different materials, as well as how hulls are put together.

Wood is the "granddaddy" of all boat construction materials. Its use dates back to the dawn of history, when men first fastened logs together and hollowed out felled tree trunks. The result of these thousands of years of experience with wood is that we know its properties quite well, and can build boats that will last for a great many years. Unlike Fiberglas and aluminum, wood is relatively easy to work. Many repairs are well within the capability of the average man who is reasonably handy with woodworking tools. Decay and rot, which attack wood but not Fiberglas and

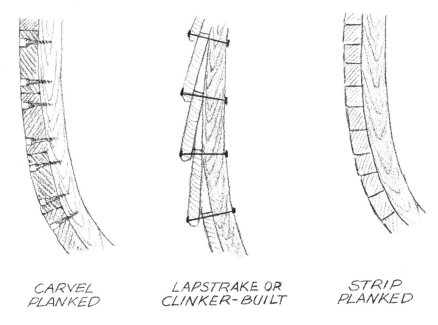

CARVEL   LAPSTRAKE OR   STRIP
PLANKED   CLINKER-BUILT   PLANKED

Figure 24. Comparison of the structural details of carvel-planked, lap-strake, and strip-planked hulls.

aluminum, are now relatively easy to control. Special wood preservatives that both prevent and stop rot are now available. They can be applied to an existing hull, or to the lumber going into a new hull at the time of construction.

Three different types of wooden hulls are now in general use: the planked hull; the flat- or V-bottomed hull constructed of waterproof plywood sheets; and the molded-plywood hull, in which the plywood sheet is shaped over a hull form.

There are three types of planked hulls. The first is known as *carvel* planked. In this type of construction the planks are fitted edge to edge over a framework of ribs or bulkheads. The seams between the planks are then caulked to make them watertight. Carvel planking can be used on V-, round-, or flat-bottomed hulls.

In the *lapstrake* or *clinker-built* type of planking, overlapping planks or strakes are riveted together to form tight seams. The planks are fastened to light ribs or frames. Boats utilizing this type of construction are usually round- or arc-bottomed and light in weight. In general, they ride better than carvel-planked boats.

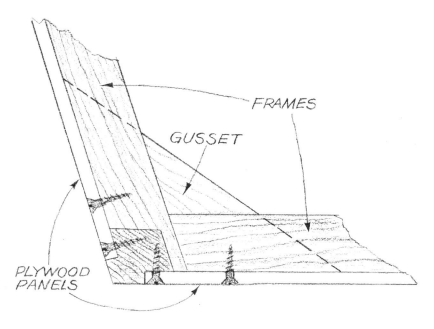

FRAMES

GUSSET

PLYWOOD
PANELS

Figure 25. How plywood-planked hulls are constructed. Hulls of this material are limited to flat or V bottoms.

In the *strip-planked* type of construction, narrow strips of wood are edge-nailed and glued to each other over structural bulkheads. Boats made this way are usually roomy and uncluttered because bulkheads take the place of ribs or frames. They are also strong and light. In addition, because of the type of construction, a strip-planked hull is essentially a one-piece hull of very great strength. Also on the plus side, there are no seams to caulk, and the interior of the hull is smooth.

Planked and caulked hulls are strong and flexible, yet they suffer from persistent and annoying leaks. Probably no other maintenance chore has gained the notoriety of caulking; most owners of wood boats are familiar with the feeling of discouragement that accompanies the tedious chore of caulking. Plywood-planked hulls are strong and durable, yet they are not satisfactory to the skipper who desires an arc- or round-bottomed hull. In addition, if they are not carefully constructed, the edges of the plywood planking may absorb water and the laminated layers become separated.

Molded-plywood hulls, on the other hand, are extremely rigid and strong. These one-piece molded sheets are so strong that ribs and frames are sometimes not necessary. With waterproof glue eliminating many metal fastenings, the net result is a lightweight, easy-to-maintain hull.

When you go out to buy a boat, you will no doubt see far more *Fiberglas* hulls than any other type. When such hulls are manufactured, the Fiberglas is laid down on permanent molds, which are then used over and over again. The hull is often molded. in one piece; the topside, consisting of deck, cabin trunk, and cockpit, is also molded in one piece. The two parts are then fastened together. As you can see, the naval architect has great freedom when Fiberglas is the hull material. It can be shaped in any manner desired. The next time you are near the water, take a closer look at some of the hull shapes on modern outboards. Speed buffs, in particular, have a very wide choice of hull configurations.

Fiberglas as a construction material is still in its youth. Experience with this substance dates back only to World War II. Indeed, it is said that the Navy is still using patrol boats molded during that war. Whatever the length of time it has been in use, however, Fiberglas seems to be an exceptionally fine hull material if it is handled properly, with strict control of the manufacturing process.

Molded Fiberglas is free from leaks, although Fiberglas boats may leak at seams, around windows, and through fittings. All seats, berths, storage spaces, flotation materials, and other units can be molded in place. Some say Fiberglas is unattractive because it lacks the warmth of wood. This is something you will have to decide for yourself when you buy, although more and more boat builders are including wood trim in the cockpits and cabins of their "glass" boats.

Despite the many good features that have led to wide use of Fiberglas, it has some serious drawbacks. Probably most important, it has very little elasticity. There is little or no "give" when it is struck a hard blow. Thus one of two possibilities exists: Either the hull resists the blow or it fractures. In addition, Fiberglas is very hard and dense. It is thus not easy to work with; repairs that might be easily made on a wood hull often stump the owner of a Fiberglas boat. Finally, the slick, glossy surface of a "glass" boat is easily gouged and scraped by the objects it routinely comes into contact with during operation. This surface, or *gelcoat,* is actually a thin layer of pigmented resin bonded to the hull. Its normal lifetime is about three years at the most. When refinishing is necessary, the whole hull must be painted, preferably with an epoxy-type marine paint.

Aluminum is just beginning to come into its own as a structural material for pleasure boats. It has been uphill all the way since the end of World War II, for at that time aluminum boats acquired a very bad reputation. A great many boats were built with surplus aircraft aluminum, which unfortunately turned out to be incompatible with seawater. The boats corroded and came apart very quickly. Today's marine aluminum alloys, on the other hand, are extremely resistant to corrosion. Boats built of these alloys have a very long corrosion-free lifetime.

In addition, improved construction techniques now produce aluminum hulls of great structural strength. Along with the fact that they are considerably lighter in weight, aluminum hulls are less susceptible than wood and Fiberglas to structural damage. Serious damage can be a problem, however, for not many boatyards are equipped to repair aluminum hulls.

If you look, you will find boats constructed of aluminum. Consider them carefully. Although they may cost a little more to purchase, they more than repay this investment with liveliness while under way, a high resale value, and simpler maintenance.

A BUYING STRATEGY

There is a certain magic about owning your own boat. Whenever you are aboard, the boat is yours alone to control. In a very real way you are the master of your destiny, be it a safe, pleasant trip or a harrowing ordeal in a gale. Prospective boat owners know this, of course. And they look forward to the very special thrill of skippering their own craft. This happy anticipation, however, can be a handicap when the purchase of a boat is being considered. Don't be carried away by your own enthusiasm, by the usually erroneous advice of well-meaning friends, by the glittering promises of brochures and advertising, by a dealer's assurances that "this is just the boat for you." Instead, approach the problem slowly and carefully, and get answers you believe you can live with to the following questions.

What should I pay? Only you can answer this question. Coming up with a meaningful answer, however, will require a careful assessment of your boating needs in light of what your purse will stand. If you're like lots of other people, your first outing in quest of a boat will be disappointing. You'll discover that the old adage about "champagne taste on a beer pocketbook" is very true indeed. If this happens, take a good hard look at what you want a boat to do for you. More often than not, there will be a way to get out on the water at a cost you can manage.

What type of boat should I buy? This should be the easiest question to answer. Presumably you have been thinking and planning for some time, and at this point know exactly how you intend to use the boat. Let's assume, for example, that father wants to fish from time to time, that the kids would rather water ski than do anything else, but that the entire family will occasionally go on picnics or day-long cruises on a fairly large lake. A runabout or utility, eighteen feet or greater in length, should satisfy all these requirements, assuming that it is adequately powered. If, on the other hand, your plans include only picnicking, swimming, and day cruising on the placid waters of a small river, a flat-topped pontoon boat may be just the thing.

Ask the right questions. You know where you plan to use the boat. Go to that locality and ask about the types of boats being used successfully. Brokers, marine supply dealers, marina and boatyard operators, Power Squadron members, and other local boating authorities are usually quite willing to share what they have learned over the years about the water and weather conditions of the region.

Try it out before you buy. Despite a dealer's or salesman's glowing promises about the performance of a boat, there is only one way to discover what it will do under operating conditions: Skipper it yourself! Either arrange with a dealer for an extended trial in a demonstrator, or charter the model (or something similar) that you are interested in. Once aboard the boat, however, remember to duplicate the conditions under which you expect to operate. The temptation will be great, with added encouragement from the dealer, to go out for a high-speed run on a calm day with just one or two people aboard. Resist this impulse, and to the best of your ability, work through each and every operating condition you anticipate. Of course, it is your money, and if you would prefer to plunk it down for an unknown commodity, go right ahead. Pause a moment, however. About how many of the thousands of used boats that go up for sale each year, do you suppose, are "unloaded" because they were purchased in haste and for the wrong reasons?

What features should I look for? It is assumed that you are interested in a planing hull, so no comment will be made on displacement hulls. Now, what features make an outboard-powered planing hull a good buy? To begin with, the hull must be of sturdy construction. Outboard hulls take a tremendous pounding, especially in choppy water, and must be built to take it. Be cautious; there are many poorly built boats available.

Look for a fairly wide transom. As pointed out earlier, the wider the transom, the greater the stability. The wide aftersection is important also with respect to planing capability. If the after end of the boat is too narrow, no amount of power will make the boat plane.

Be sure the hull has a sturdy rub rail. Outboards take a lot of bumping and scraping during use. The rub rail absorbs some of the shock of the bumps, and also protects the rest of the hull from scrapes and gouges.

Don't go overboard for fancy bright metal. Those shiny cleats, clocks, instrument dials, and other goodies look great in a showroom, but out on the water they must be polished to stay bright. Unless you have nothing better to do, avoid these chores.

Look for a modest amount of flare in the bow section of the boat. This will divert water downward and outward away from the boat when planing, instead of back into the cockpit. An overly wet ride takes all the fun out of boating.

The best all-purpose hull shape? No hull can be all things to all people; nevertheless, it is possible to single out what is for most people the most practical hull shape. This is the V-bottomed planing hull, with a medium flare at the bow. The V-hull shape gives directional stability, handles well at displacement speeds, and planes nicely at higher speeds.

Should I buy a new or used boat? This decision is entirely up to you. If you buy a new boat, you will probably pay more for what you get, but the boat and engine will be covered by a guarantee. Keep in mind, too, that it is in the dealer's best interest to honor the guarantee cheerfully and without undue delays. He wants your good will, for he knows that the majority of boat owners "move up" sooner or later. He'd like to sell you that larger boat each time you make a change.

If you shop carefully, knowing precisely what you want before venturing into the market, you should be able to make a good buy on a used boat. Assuming this is the case, you can probably count on getting more for your money than in a new boat. The boat you pick up should be larger and carry more power for the money than a new boat.

It is very important, however, that you determine the exact condition of any boat being considered. This is *not* done by a superficial inspection of hull and fittings, and a five-minute audition of an engine running in a barrel. Many's the man who has said, "It looks and sounds okay to me," only to be sorry later. Instead, there is a well-established approach that eliminates most of the hazards of used-boat buying and should find you a good buy.

The first step is to deal with a reputable broker. Avoid buying from someone who is neither a broker nor a dealer. Stay away from that fabulous deal you heard about from a friend who in turn heard about it from someone at the office. Explain your needs carefully to the broker you have selected, and respect his recommendations. If he is to maintain his reputation for integrity (and, incidentally, capture your trade-in business when the time comes), he will not give you a bum steer.

When you have selected a boat you feel fits your needs, the next step is to arrange a survey. Never buy a used boat without having it surveyed. The survey is a comprehensive but impartial evaluation of the condition of the boat and engine, carried out by a professional. For this service, you, the prospective buyer, pay the fee. You get for your money a detailed statement of what is wrong with the boat and engine. If the survey gives the boat a clean bill of health, you're on your way. If not, you are in a position to price needed repairs and then make a judgment about the asking price on the boat.

No matter how you look at it, the money spent for a survey is the most important investment you will make in a used boat. It is, quite simply, the difference between the joy of a good boat and the agony of a clunker.

3. NAUTICAL TERMINOLOGY

BEFORE WE GO ANY FARTHER, it is necessary that you become familiar with those nautical terms used most frequently by boating enthusiasts. As we progress into the numerous details of boat operation and handling, these terms will be used repeatedly. Thus, to follow the text with understanding, you should become familiar with the Glossary that follows, and then refer to it whenever you are in doubt about the meaning of a term.

Your first task is to learn the names and functions of the major parts of an outboard-powered boat. Although this is no easy chore for someone who has little or no experience with boating, it is necessary if you are to master the skills needed to get you out on the water. Refer to Figure 26. These are the most important parts of an outboard. All these terms are included in the Glossary. Look them up now one by one, and try to remember the description and purpose of each. Then, as you read on, take the time to refer back to the Glossary whenever you are unsure of the meaning of a term.

Although this is not a book on sailing, a diagram showing the structural parts of a typical small sailboat is included (Figure 29); in addition, the terms are listed in the Glossary. This is done to permit you to become familiar with basic sailboat terminology. After all, no boatman worth his salt wants to be ignorant of the rig the other person is using. Moreover, who can predict what your interests may be in the future? As thousands before you have, you may develop a desire to learn how to sail. If you do, it will help to know the parts of a sailboat before getting started.

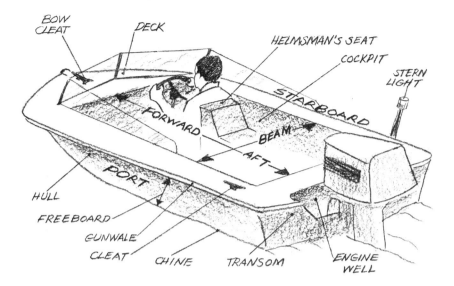

Figure 26. The nautical terms for the major parts of an outboard-powered boat. Each term is listed in the Glossary.

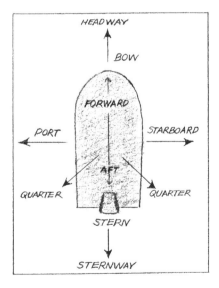

Figure 27. Terms used to indicate direction from a position facing forward on a boat.

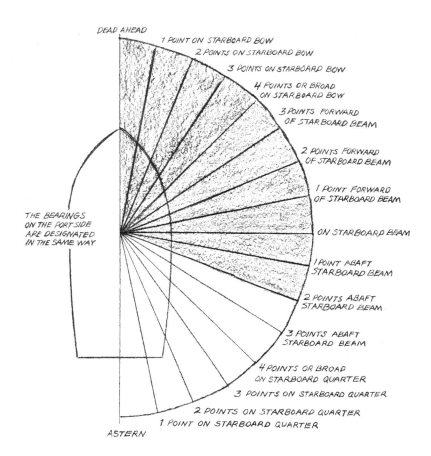

Figure 28. Directions and bearings from aboard a boat. One point equals 11.25 degrees, and each point is named. The shaded zone, from dead ahead to two points abaft the starboard beam, is called the danger zone. See the rules of the road.

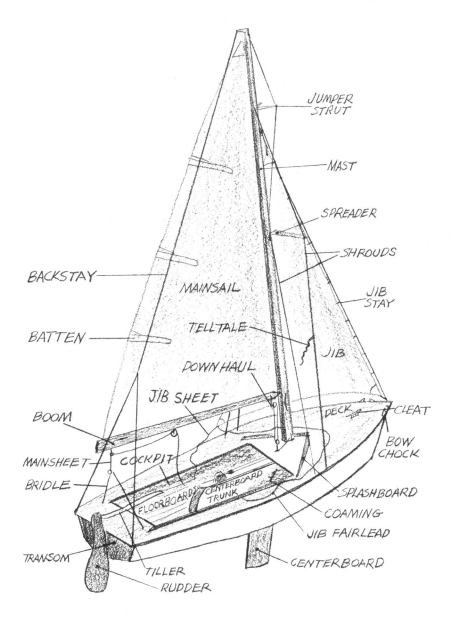

Figure 29. The anatomy of a centerboard-type daysailer.

GLOSSARY

ABAFT: aft; "abaft the beam," for example, is aft of the beam.

ABEAM: off the side of a boat at an angle of ninety degrees to the fore-and-aft centerline.

AFT: in the direction of the stern.

AHEAD: in the direction of the vessel's bow.

ALEE: away from the direction of the wind.

AMIDSHIPS: at the center of a vessel, in terms of either length or width.

ANCHOR: an iron or steel device designed to hold a vessel in place when dropped to the bottom.

ANCHORAGE: a suitable place for dropping anchor.

ASTERN: in the direction of the vessel's stern.

BACKSTAY: a wire-rope mast support leading aft from the top of a mast to the deck or to another mast.

BALLAST: heavy weight placed at or near the bottom of a sailboat to provide stability.

BAROMETER: an instrument that measures atmospheric pressure.

BATTENS: thin rigid strips that fit into pockets along the after edge of a sail; battens help to hold the shape of a sail.

BEAM: the greatest width of a vessel, usually amidships.

BEAM ENDS: the ends of a vessel's beams, which lie parallel to the deck; when a ship is on its beam ends, it is tipped so much to one side that its beams approach the vertical.

BEAM WIND: a wind blowing at right angles to the fore-and-aft centerline of a vessel.

BEARING: the direction of an object from a vessel relative to the vessel's heading, or by compass.

BEARING: directions from aboard a boat; see Figure 28.

BELOW: toward the lower portion of a vessel.

BEND: to fasten one rope to another; also to fasten a sail to the boom and mast.

BILGE: the portion of the inside hull below the floorboards.

BOOM: spar at the bottom of a mainsail or mizzensail on sloops, yawls, and ketches, and other sailing vessels.

BOOM CRUTCH: a support that holds the boom off the deck when it is not in use.

BOW: the forward part of the hull of a vessel.

BOW CHOCKS: metal fittings situated on either side of the bow that lead anchor or mooring lines inboard.

BOWLINE: a knot used to form a loop at the end of a line.

BREAKWATER: a sea wall that breaks the force of waves.

BRIDLE: a span of rope to which the mainsheet, and sometimes the spinnaker pole, are attached.

BRIGHTWORK: varnished woodwork and polished brass aboard a vessel.

BRISTOL FASHION: in a seamanlike manner.

BROACH: to swing around and position the vessel broadside to wind and waves.

BUOY: a floating marker used for piloting; see *can buoy* and *nun buoy*.

BURDENED VESSEL: a vessel required by law to stay clear of another vessel holding the right of way.

CAN BUOY: a black cylindrical buoy carrying an odd number that marks the left, or port side of a channel when a vessel is approaching from seaward.

CAPSIZE: to overturn.

CAST OFF: to release a line; in general, to let go all lines and leave a dock.

CATAMARAN: a twin-hulled vessel.

CENTERBOARD: a hinged plate housed in a trunk or well along the centerline of a sailboat, and lowered below the bottom of the hull to reduce leeway when sailing to windward.

CENTERBOARD TRUNK: the housing for a centerboard when it is not lowered into place.

CHAIN PLATES: metal straps bolted to the side of a vessel that secure the shrouds.

CHART: a nautical map.

CHINE: intersection of a hull's side and bottom.

CHOCK: a metal fitting that leads lines over the side of a vessel.

CLEAT: a horn-shaped fitting used to secure a line.

CLOVE HITCH: two half hitches thrown around a spar or another rope.

COAMING: raised railing around a cockpit to prevent water from running in.

COCKPIT: opening at after end of a boat for passengers.

COIL: to lay a rope in a circular pattern.

COMPASS COURSE: a vessel's heading based on the vessel's compass.

COMPASS ROSE: a graduated circle carrying the points of the compass and printed on a chart.

COURSE: the heading of a vessel as indicated by the compass.

CRUISER: when outboard-powered, a boat generally less than twenty-five feet in length with Spartan living accommodations.

CUDDY: a small shelter cabin forward of the cockpit.

CURRENT: the horizontal movement of water caused by tide, wind, or gravity.

DECK: the floor or horizontal surface of a vessel.

DEVIATION: the effect of iron objects or electrical equipment on the compass reading.

DINGHY (DINK):   a small open boat.

DISPLACEMENT: the weight of water displaced by a vessel; thus the vessel's own weight.

DRAFT: the depth of water needed to float a vessel.

EBB TIDE: the tide during its passage from high to low water.

EVEN KEEL: floating level, not heeled over or listing.

EYE OF THE WIND: the exact direction from which the wind is coming.

EYE SPLICE: a loop spliced in the end of a rope.

FATHOM: a unit of measure equal to six feet.

FENDER: a cushion that prevents a boat's side from striking a dock or the side of another boat.

FIGURE-EIGHT KNOT: a knot tied in the end of a line to prevent it from running through a block.

FISHERMAN'S BEND: a knot used for making the anchor line fast to the anchor.

FLOOD TIDE: the tide during its passage from low to high water.

FLOORBOARDS: planking on the bottom of the cockpit.

FLOTSAM: floating debris.

FOGBOUND: held in port or at anchor because of fog.

FORWARD: in front of, as in "forward of the beam."

FOUL: snarl or tangle; the opposite of clear.

FOUND: furnished; a vessel is said to be "well found" if it is well equipped.

FREEBOARD: the distance from the top of the hull to the water.

GOOSENECK: the fitting that fastens the boom to the mast on a sailboat.

GROUND SWELL: long waves coming from seaward.

GROUND TACKLE: a term used to cover all anchor and mooring gear.

GUNWALE: the rail of a vessel at deck level.

HALF HITCH: a turn around a spar or rope with the end coming through the bight (the bight is the portion of the rope between the ends).

HALYARDS: lines used to hoist the sails.

HAUL: to pull on a line; also said of wind that has shifted toward the bow.

HEADSAILS: all sails set forward of the foremast (the single mast on a sloop).

HEADSTAY: a wire-rope mast support running from the top or near the top of the mast to the bow.

HEAD UP: to point the bow of the vessel more nearly into the wind.

HEADWAY: motion ahead.

HEAVE: to throw, as in "heave a line"; also the rise and fall of a vessel in a seaway.

HEEL: to tip or list to one side.

HELM: the tiller or wheel.

HITCH: a method of making a rope fast to another object.

HOUSEBOAT: a "floating miniature apartment"; these craft may be powered by an outboard, inboard-outboard, or inboard engine.

HULL SPEED: maximum speed of a displacement hull; determined by hull shape and waterline length.

INSHORE: toward the shore.

JETSAM: articles thrown overboard that sink or wash ashore.

JETTISON: to throw overboard.

JIB: a triangular sail set forward of the foremast (the single mast on a sloop).

JIBSHEET: the line from the lower aft end of the jib to the cockpit; used to control the set of the jib.

JIBSTAY: the forward stay, or forestay, to which the leading edge of the jib is attached.

JUMPER STRUT: a strut aloft on the forward side of the mast for added support.

JURY RIG: any makeshift rig.

KEDGE: a small anchor used for warping (pulling) a vessel forward.

KEDGING OUT: to free a vessel aground or move away from a lee dock by hauling on a kedge anchor.

KEEL: the fore-and-aft backbone timber along the centerline of a vessel; on keel sailboats, the keel extends well below the rest of the hull and provides weight stability and lateral resistance.

KNOCKDOWN: when a vessel is thrown on its beam ends by a sudden gust of wind.

KNOT: a measure of speed meaning *nautical mile per hour* (one nautical mile equals 6,080.20 feet); also a method of binding objects together using rope.

LAND BREEZE: a breeze blowing from land to sea.

LANDLUBBER: seaman's term for a person unfamiliar with the sea and seafaring.

LATITUDE: angular distance north or south from the equator.

LAZARETTE: below-deck storage space aft.

LEEWARD: away from the direction of the wind.

LEEWAY: sideways motion of a boat; often caused by wind, waves, or current.

LINES: ropes on a vessel that are used for special purposes, such as *sheet lines, bow lines,* or *guy lines.*

LONGITUDE: angular distance from the prime meridian (which passes through Greenwich, England).

LOWER UNIT: the driveshaft, gears, and propeller of an outboard or inboard-outboard unit.

MAGNETIC BEARING: the compass direction of an object from a vessel.

MAGNETIC COURSE: the heading of a vessel based on the magnetic compass.

MAINSAIL: fore-and-aft sail set on the after side of the mainmast.

MAINSHEET: the line from the main boom to the cockpit; used to control the set of the mainsail.

MARLINSPIKE: a pointed tool used for separating rope or wire strands when splicing.

MAST: a vertical spar that supports other spars, rigging, and sails.

MASTHEAD: the top of the mast; a rig in which the headsails extend to the top of the mast.

MOORING: a large, permanent anchor and buoy; generally a vessel's permanent home.

NAUTICAL MILE: a unit of distance equal to 6,080.20 feet; see *knot.*

NUN BUOY: a conical red buoy carrying an even number and marking the right, or starboard side of a channel entering from seaward.

OFFSHORE: away from the shore.

OUTBOARD: beyond the side of a vessel.

PAINTER: a short length of rope attached to the bow of a small boat.

PAY OUT: to ease or feed out a rope.

PENNANT: a small narrow flag; also the length of rope that attaches a vessel to its mooring float.

PLANE: to skim along the surface of the water.

POINT: a unit of angular measure; one point equals 11.25 degrees; see *bearings*.

PORT: the left side of a vessel facing forward.

POWERHEAD: the cylinder(s), spark plug(s), carburetor, ignition system, and related parts of an outboard engine.

PRAM: a small dinghy having square ends.

PRIVILEGED VESSEL: the vessel holding the right of way; the *burdened vessel* must keep clear.

RAIL: the outer edge of the deck on a vessel.

RIGHT: to return a vessel to its normal position, as in "righting a capsized boat."

RIGHT OF WAY: the right of the privileged vessel to hold course and speed.

RODE: the anchor line or cable.

RUDDER: the flat plate hinged at or near the stern below the waterline that is used to steer a vessel; the rudder is controlled by the *tiller* or *wheel*.

RULES OF THE ROAD: the laws of navigation; their primary purpose is the avoidance of collisions.

RUNABOUT: a well-equipped open power boat in the fifteen-to-twenty-foot range.

SCOPE: the length of anchor line let out.

SEA ANCHOR: a dragging device used to slow a vessel down in heavy weather.

SEA BREEZE: a breeze blowing from sea to land.

SEAWAY: an area of sea with moderate or heavy seas running.

SEAWORTHY: capable of putting to sea and meeting sea conditions.

SHEET: a line that controls the set of the sails; see *jibsheet* and *mainsheet*.

SHIPSHAPE: neat and seamanlike.

SHOVE OFF: to depart.

SHROUDS: the rigging that supports a mast at its sides.

SKEG: extension of the keel protecting the propeller.

SLOOP: a one-masted sailboat, carrying mainsail and jib.

SNUB: to check or stop a rope suddenly.

SPAR: a term applied to masts, booms, gaffs, etc.

SPLASHBOARD: a raised board on deck designed to deflect spray away from the cockpit.

SPLICE: a method for weaving strands of rope together.

SPREADER: a horizontal strut to which shrouds are attached to support the mast.

SPRING LINE: a dock line leading forward or aft that keeps a vessel from moving astern or ahead.

SQUALL: a sudden and violent local storm or gust of wind.

SQUARE KNOT: a knot consisting of two overhand knots.

STANDING RIGGING: the part of a sailboat's rigging, that is, the *shrouds* and *stays,* that support the mast.

STARBOARD: the right side of a vessel facing forward.

STAYS: the rigging running forward and aft that supports the mast; see *backstay, headstay,* and *jibstay.*

STEERAGE WAY: enough headway to permit steering.

STERN: the after end of a vessel.

STERNWAY: motion astern.

STOW: to store away on a vessel.

SWAMP: to sink by filling with water.

TACKLE: a combination of blocks and rope—a "block and tackle."

TAUT: having no slack.

TELLTALE: a strip of ribbon or yarn tied to a shroud to show the apparent direction of the wind.

TENDER: lacking stability; also a small boat used for ferrying passengers.

THWARTSHIPS: at right angles to the fore-and-aft line on a vessel; from side to side.

TIDE: the rise and fall of the sea level.

TIDE RIPS: areas of disturbed and turbulent water caused by strong tidal currents.

TILLER: a rod used to control the rudder.

TOPSIDE: on deck.

TOPSIDES: the sides of a vessel between the waterline and the rail.

TRANSOM: the stern planking of a square-sterned vessel.

TRIM: the fore-and-aft balance of a vessel; also to adjust the sails to take best advantage of the wind.

TRUE COURSE: a course that has been corrected for variation and deviation.

TURNBUCKLE: a thread-and-screw device used to adjust the tension in shrouds and stays.

UNDER WAY: in motion and under control of the helmsman.

UP ANCHOR: the command to raise the anchor and get under way.

UTILITY: a stripped-down open boat in the ten-to-fifteen-foot range.

VARIATION: the local differences in degrees between true north and magnetic north.

VEER: when the wind changes direction toward the stern.

WAKE: the track a vessel leaves astern as it passes through the water.

WATERLINE: a line painted on a vessel's side to indicate its proper trim.

WEATHER SIDE: the windward side.

WELL FOUND: a well-equipped vessel with all gear in good condition.

WHIPPING: twine or thread wound around the end of a rope to keep it from fraying.

WINCH: a mechanical device used to haul lines.

WINDWARD: toward the wind; the weather side of a vessel.

YACHT: any vessel designed for pleasure use.

YAW: to steer uncontrollably out of the line of the course, as when running with a heavy quartering sea.

4. OUTBOARD ENGINES—I

ON ANY GIVEN DAY during the boating season, literally thousands of people—be they fishermen, kids water skiing, a family off on a picnic, or what have you—simply jump into their boats, push the starter button or yank the starter cord, and take off with the engine purring. Their confidence is obvious. They know that barring trouble of an extraordinary nature, their outboard engines will get them there and back safely and efficiently.

An adman's dream? Or the real world of outboarding? Rest easy. Given the reasonable and systematic care any machine requires, this is truly the real world of outboarding. There are very few mechanical devices that can take as much abuse and still give the top-notch service of a modern outboard engine.

Clearly, however, one cannot expect unlimited trouble-free performance from an outboard if normal maintenance procedures are not followed. The key here is normal, routine care. Call it preventive maintenance, if you like. But whatever the term, we are talking about a rather limited number of procedures that, if followed religiously, come very close to guaranteeing unlimited trouble-free performance. But more about maintenance procedures later.

At this point you have learned something about the types of outboard boats available, as well as something about the design and performance characteristics of outboard hulls. It's time now to come to grips with the problem of matching an engine to the boat of your choice.

MATCHING ENGINE TO BOAT

No decision you will make with respect to buying and fitting out an outboard-powered boat is as important as the choice of an engine; to be more specific, the choice of an engine whose power output matches the requirements of the hull you have selected. It is important from the standpoint of performance to do better than just make sure that the boat is not overpowered. An overpowered hull can be very dangerous, to be sure. An underpowered hull, on the other hand, will perform sluggishly and inefficiently. Thus the task boils down to determining the power needed to give maximum safe performance.

Make a careful check of the hull you have selected. It will probably carry a special plate giving the hull's power and load limits. If the plate has not been provided, a procedure worked out by the Boating Industry Association will do the job. This calculation gives the maximum safe horsepower capacity of the hull when operated by the average person for family boating purposes. See Figure 30. This table relates a computed boat-size factor to horsepower capacity.

The first step is to compute the factor by multiplying the over-all boat length in feet by the over-all stern width in feet. This is the width of the widest part of the stern excluding fins and sheer. The second step is to locate the factor and the corresponding horsepower capacity in Figure 30. If the resultant horsepower capacity is not a multiple of five, it may be raised to the next multiple of five. For example, if the factor for a boat is 41, the horsepower capacity is 10. Suppose the factor is 74 and the boat has a 20-inch transom and remote steering. This calculation is (2×74) $-90 = 58$. The horsepower capacity of this hull is therefore 60.

One final point about selecting an engine. A logical source of information is the builder of your hull. If you are at all in doubt, ask him. If he is a reputable builder, he will have conducted extensive tests on your hull type using a variety of power options. Be sure to tell him, however, how many people and how much gear you will normally expect to carry.

At this point, if you have spent any time near or on the water, you're probably wondering whether you should power your boat with one or two engines. Outboard craft powered by two engines do seem to outrun the rest of the pack, although this feeling could be the result of an overactive imagination. In any event, the choice of one or two engines is a legitimate question and deserves a reasonable answer.

To begin with, let's see what you can expect to get with two engines. Speed, contrary to the hopes of some wild-eyed enthusiasts, does not

Multiply overall length_____ x stern width_____ = factor_____
(nearest whole number)

	thru 35	36-39	40-42	43-45	46-49	50-53	54-57	Remote steering and 20" Transom or equivalent	No remote steering or Transom less than 20" or equivalent
								over 57	over 57
If this factor is	thru 35	36-39	40-42	43-45	46-49	50-53	54-57	over 57	over 57
H.P. capacity is	3	5	7½	10	15	20	25	(2 x factor) −90	(¾ factor) −20

H.P. capacity =_____ (raise to even 5 horsepower increment)

Reduce horsepower 50% for flat bottom hard chine boats.

Figure 30. How boat-size factor is related to maximum safe horsepower for a hull. See the text for details.

double. Depending upon the power of the engines and other factors, the boat's maximum speed will increase by 25 to 35 per cent—no more. Fuel consumption increases, of course, but not as much as you might think. It is true that the number of gallons burned per hour will double, but when the range of the boat is taken into consideration, actual fuel cost is increased by only 25 to 30 per cent.

The safety factor is a definite plus with two engines. Any skipper planning to travel long distances should give serious consideration to two engines, if only because of the added safety. The second engine will always get you home if the first one conks out. Some boats carry a smaller second engine for trolling. This too is useful if the larger engine quits. Don't make the mistake many boatmen make with this type of rig, however. If the smaller engine is rarely used and rarely serviced, it may fail to operate just when it is needed most.

Now, what are the disadvantages of twin engines? With all power components doubled, space may become a problem. In smaller boats, in particular, the passenger space remaining can be very limited indeed. Lower unit drag will be doubled, of course, because two lower units are immersed in the water. In addition, the added weight of the second power unit and gasoline tank, plus the increased drag, combine to make the boat float lower in the water and take longer to reach planing speeds. Finally, the boat will be carrying twice as much fuel. It is said that one-half pint of gasoline has the destructive power of five sticks of dynamite. On this basis alone, some feel that doubling the fuel load is a questionable practice.

ANATOMY OF AN OUTBOARD

If you are to make the most of what outboard engines offer, it is necessary to know something about their mechanical construction and operation. Like automobile engines, outboards require a certain amount of care.
Without this care there can be a high risk of engine failure. Moreover,
while the motorist usually finds help relatively easily, this is most often
not the case when a marine engine fails. How does a boatman find a
mechanic in the middle of a large lake or three miles off Montauk Point?
The answer is, he doesn't. First he gets a tow into port, often after
several hours of drifting, and then he looks for the mechanic. In any
event, engine failure on a boat invariably ruins the outing planned. But
this need not be. With reasonable care most outboards are remarkably
reliable and will give hour after hour of steady, trouble-free service. Take
care of your outboard engine and it will take care of you.

Regardless of power rating, size, shape, or price, all outboard engines
consist of a *powerhead* and a *lower unit.* See Figure 31. The powerhead,
as the name implies, consists of the engine proper—that is, the cylinder(s),
spark plug(s), carburetor, and ignition system. It is here that the stored
energy of the fuel is converted to the mechanical energy of motion (the
spinning propeller) that powers the boat. The lower unit consists of a
driveshaft, gears, and the propeller. The driveshaft and gears transmit the
mechanical energy produced by combustion of the fuel to the propeller.

As in all internal combustion engines, the three fundamental systems of
an outboard are the *fuel system,* the *ignition system,* and the *cooling system.* The fuel system stores and then delivers fuel in combustible form to
the combustion chambers—the cylinders. The fuel—usually gasoline—is
stored in a small tank attached to the engine on smaller engines. For
larger engines, the fuel is stored in a separate tank. This tank may be
portable, or it may be built into the hull of the boat. Regardless of how
the fuel is stored, however, it is fed through a carburetor to the cylinders.
The carburetor mixes the vaporized fuel with air and feeds this combustible mixture to the cylinders.

The ignition system is nothing more nor less than a method for producing a hot spark inside the cylinder at just the right moment. This
moment is the point at which burning the fuel-air mixture yields the
greatest amount of mechanical energy. The spark, of course, is delivered
by the spark plug, which is mounted through the wall of the cylinder. An
important part of the function of the ignition system is timing the spark.

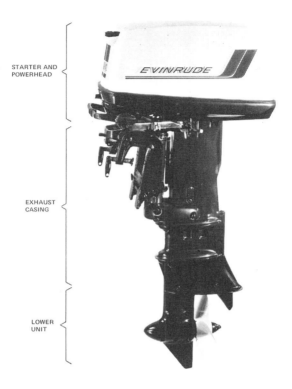

STARTER AND
POWERHEAD

EXHAUST
CASING

LOWER
UNIT

Figure 31. The external anatomy of an outboard engine, in this case Evinrude's 40-hp Norseman. (*Photo courtesy of Evinrude Motors.*)

If it should occur at any point other than the moment of maximum power generation, the engine will perform sluggishly (or not at all) and deliver less power than it is capable of.

It is a fact of life that not all the energy released by the combustion of the fuel appears as mechanical power at the propeller. A large portion of this energy appears as heat and is wasted, for the heat serves no useful purpose in terms of propelling the boat. Excessive heat is the enemy of efficient engine operation, for it accelerates the corrosion of metallic parts. It also causes the expansion of metal and therefore increases friction between metallic parts that move in relation to each other. The most important of these parts are the pistons and the cylinder walls. When the

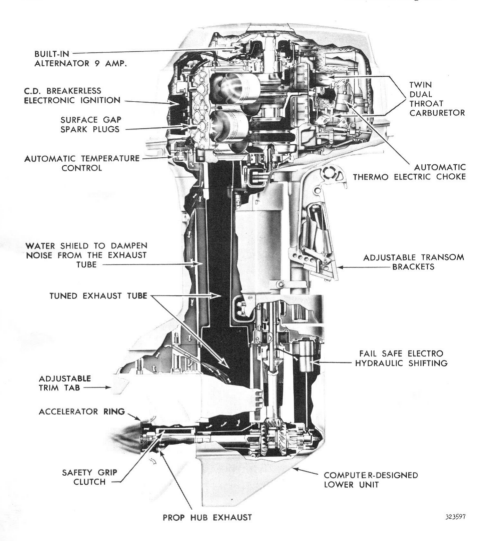

BUILT-IN ALTERNATOR 9 AMP.

C.D. BREAKERLESS ELECTRONIC IGNITION

SURFACE GAP SPARK PLUGS

AUTOMATIC TEMPERATURE CONTROL

WATER SHIELD TO DAMPEN NOISE FROM THE EXHAUST TUBE

TUNED EXHAUST TUBE

ADJUSTABLE TRIM TAB

ACCELERATOR RING

SAFETY GRIP CLUTCH

PROP HUB EXHAUST

TWIN DUAL THROAT CARBURETOR

AUTOMATIC THERMO ELECTRIC CHOKE

ADJUSTABLE TRANSOM BRACKETS

FAIL SAFE ELECTRO HYDRAULIC SHIFTING

COMPUTER-DESIGNED LOWER UNIT

323597

Figure 32. Cutaway of an outboard engine showing the major internal parts. The pistons are just to the right of the spark plugs. The driveshaft runs vertically from the crankshaft behind the pistons down to the gear case in the lower unit. (*Photo courtesy of Evinrude Motors.*)

fuel-air mixture burns it expands, forcing the piston out of the cylinder. It is this linear motion of the piston that is converted to circular motion in the driveshaft.

When an engine overheats, expansion tightens the fit between piston and cylinder wall. If overheating continues unchecked, the excessive friction produced can literally "weld" the piston to the cylinder wall. When this happens, the engine is said to have "frozen up."

Clearly, if an engine is not to overheat, excess heat must be carried away. This is accomplished by the cooling system, which takes advantage of the unlimited supply of cool water available outside the engine. Most outboards contain a small pump that drives the cool water through the engine's cooling system to an exhaust vent. As the water circulates, it absorbs excess heat and carries it away from the engine. A *thermostat* built into the cooling system regulates the rate of flow of the water and therefore controls the operating temperature of the engine. Outboard engines should never be run out of the water, if it can be avoided. Without the cooling effect of water, they overheat very rapidly.

All engines must be lubricated. Outboards are no exception. Unlike automobile engines, however, which use a reservoir of oil as a source of lubricant, all but one or two outboard engines require that the oil be added to the gasoline. This, of course, eliminates the bulky and messy oil pan of the automobile engine. When the oil-gasoline mixture in an outboard reaches the cylinders, the gasoline has been vaporized to form a highly combustible gaseous mixture with the air that was drawn in through the carburetor. The oil does not vaporize, however, and lubricates cylinder walls, engine bearings, and other moving parts.

Automobile engines are four-cycle engines—only one stroke of the piston in four is a power stroke. All outboard engines, however, except for the two mentioned above and the newly introduced Wankel, or rotary-type engine, are two-cycle engines—one in every two strokes is a power stroke. Just two piston strokes—one up, one down—are required to produce a complete revolution of the crankshaft. Follow along in Figure 33 as the two-cycle sequence for a typical outboard is described.

As shown, the piston is attached to a rod, which in turn is attached to the crankshaft. These parts are connected together mechanically so that when the piston moves up and down the crankshaft rotates. This rotation is then transmitted to the propeller via the driveshaft gear box in the lower unit.

In Figure 33(A) the piston has just completed a power stroke. In moving downward, however, it has opened both the exhaust and the intake ports. The exhaust gases, still under high pressure from the explosive combustion of the fuel, flow out through the exhaust port. Prior to this stroke, however, a new fuel-air mixture had been introduced into the crankcase and sealed off by the closing of the leaf valve. Thus, as the piston thrust downward during the power stroke, the fresh fuel-air mixture was compressed. Being under pressure, it then surges into the cylinder when the intake port opens, and in fact helps to flush out the remaining exhaust gases.

The second phase of the two-cycle sequence is the compression stroke [Figure 33(B)]. During this stroke the fresh fuel-air mixture is compressed prior to being ignited. Note how the ports are closed off as the piston rises. At the same time, however, the leaf valve opens and a new charge of vaporized fuel and air enters the crankcase.

At the top of the compression stroke the fuel-air mixture in the cylinder has been reduced to the smallest possible volume. At just this point the spark plug delivers a spark, and the fuel explodes. The rapid and forceful expansion of the exploding gases then drives the piston downward in a power stroke [Figure 33(C)]. But this compresses the new fuel-air mixture in the crankcase and then opens the exhaust and intake ports. The cycle then repeats itself.

CHOOSING A PROPELLER

To obtain maximum performance from an outboard engine, the correct propeller for the conditions of use must be chosen. But this does not mean that a separate propeller should be mounted for every different load and use condition. Instead, a compromise is sought to satisfy the *average* conditions under which the boat will be used. No single propeller will be just right for every condition of operation. It is possible, however, to choose a propeller that will perform well most of the time.

The propeller converts the power generated by an engine into thrust, or drive. In this sense it is comparable to the transmission of an automobile. On most outboards the gear ratio is about one to two—the propeller turns at a rate approximately one half the revolutions per minute (rpm) produced by the engine. But to operate efficiently, the engine must be run within a given rpm range. Assuming that an engine is capable of

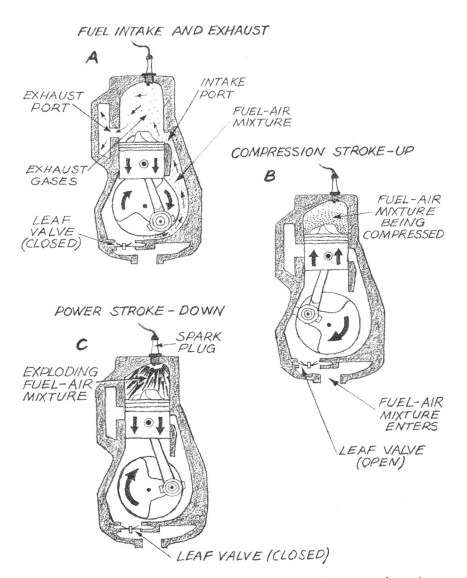

FUEL INTAKE AND EXHAUST

A

EXHAUST PORT

INTAKE PORT

FUEL-AIR MIXTURE

EXHAUST GASES

LEAF VALVE (CLOSED)

COMPRESSION STROKE-UP

B

FUEL-AIR MIXTURE BEING COMPRESSED

POWER STROKE - DOWN

C

SPARK PLUG

EXPLODING FUEL-AIR MIXTURE

FUEL-AIR MIXTURE ENTERS

LEAF VALVE (OPEN)

LEAF VALVE (CLOSED)

Figure 33. The sequence of events in the cylinder of a two-cycle engine. One in every two strokes of the piston is a power stroke. See the text for details.

producing its rated horsepower (have this checked on a tachometer at a reliable service shop), the propeller chosen will determine if it will operate properly when under load.

When an engine is operated either above or below its given rpm range, it will not produce its full rated horsepower. This can lead to serious consequences. Engines operated below their given rpm range are being overloaded. Carbon builds up in the cylinders, spark plugs foul and burn out faster, fuel economy drops, and damage can occur to the pistons and cylinder walls. Engines operated above the rated rpm range, on the other hand, simply wear out in a hurry. Little or no extra power, however, is gained by this tactic.

The *diameter* and *pitch* of a propeller can be varied to obtain the desired performance from an engine. The diameter is the distance from blade tip to blade tip. Pitch is related to the angle of attack of the propeller blades. A propeller with a fifteen-inch pitch, for example, should move the boat nearly fifteen inches through the water for each revolution.

The diameter of the propeller determines the rpm of the engine. Thus, other factors being equal, a small-diameter propeller permits higher engine speeds than a large-diameter propeller. If your engine is running below its rated rpm range, use a propeller with a smaller diameter. Pitch, on the other hand, determines how fast the boat will go for a given rpm. For maximum speed, use the largest pitch available for the correct diameter. To move the boat slowly, but maintain engine speed at or near its rated rpm, use the smallest pitch available for the correct diameter.

Another factor in propeller performance is the number of blades. Clearly, the more blades on a propeller the greater the thrust it will produce. Take a look at the different propellers in use when you have the opportunity. You will notice that when speed is desired, the propeller is often two-bladed with maximum pitch. When heavy loads are being pushed, however, a three-bladed propeller with minimum pitch is preferred. Auxiliary sailboats powered by outboards, for example, usually use the three-bladed, low-pitch propeller (unless the skipper has unwisely decided to ignore the question of propeller choice).

There are several ways to go about choosing a propeller or propellers. First, you can check with the manufacturer of your engine. Give him the structural specifications of your boat, as well as the average conditions under which you plan to use the boat. He should be able to suggest a propeller that will meet your needs. In fact, you will probably find that your

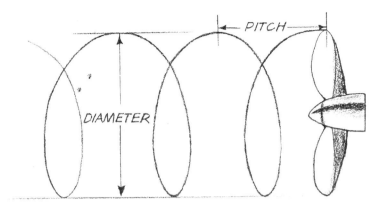

Figure 34. The relationship between the diameter and pitch of a propeller.

dealer has a large chart showing the manufacturer's recommendations, plus some pretty firm ideas of his own.

The ultimate, of course, is the two-phase test alluded to earlier. The first step is verification on a tachometer that the engine does in fact produce its rated horsepower at a given rpm. The second step is then a series of trial runs on the boat, using a variety of propellers. By elimination the propeller that gives the best engine performance for "average" load conditions is then chosen.

QUICK STARTS AND SMOOTH OPERATION

Outboard engines are similar to automobile engines in that gasoline vapor is mixed with air and then burned to yield power. The similarity ends at this point, however, for outboard engines operate differently, and of course perform a very different service. Moreover, the need to maintain running efficiency is more critical with outboard engines. As suggested earlier, the boatman wants assurance that his engine will start quickly and run smoothly for as long as he needs it.

Assuring quick starts and smooth operation is largely a matter of understanding how an outboard engine operates. There are four basic points to review and remember. First, since the lubricating oil is carried to the engine parts dissolved in the fuel, the proper mixture of oil and gasoline must be rigorously controlled. Too little oil or the wrong type of oil can lead to damaged engine parts and a drop in performance efficiency. Too much oil will foul spark plugs and prevent easy starts.

Second, the vaporized gasoline and air mixture must be fed into the cylinders in the proper explosive proportions. This is accomplished by a correctly adjusted carburetor. Unless you are an accomplished mechanic, do not attempt to go beyond the carburetor adjustments explained in the owner's manual supplied with the engine.

The third basic of efficient operation is compression. If the fuel-air mixture does not compress because of leakage around a loose spark plug, between the piston and cylinder wall, or perhaps through a crack in the cylinder head, ignition and combustion are unlikely to occur. These parts must all be kept in good mechanical condition to assure trouble-free operation.

Finally, a vigorous hot spark is needed to ignite the fuel-air mixture at just the right moment. Use the type of spark plug recommended for the conditions under which the boat is to be operated, and keep it clean. Most ignition troubles can be traced to fouled plugs. A spare set of clean and properly gapped plugs is the solution to the problem of plug failure. But don't overlook routine inspection, cleaning, and replacement of plugs when needed.

5. OUTBOARD ENGINES—II

To keep your outboard engine on the go, to guarantee quick starts and smooth trouble-free operation, regular service is a must. "That's fine," you say, "I'll plan to have it taken care of in a good shop." Simple enough, but it isn't as easy to take an outboard in for servicing as an automobile. Moreover, servicing in a shop is required perhaps once a year at the most—if you, the owner, will assume responsibility for routine preventive maintenance. As a matter of fact, you have little choice in the matter. To keep your engine performing in a safe and reliable manner, there are certain chores you must perform yourself. Stop to consider for a moment just how annoying and difficult it would be to turn to professional help every time something has to be done to an engine. You could wind up spending more time at the shop than on the water. Instead, make it a point to learn the routine tasks needed to keep an engine operating at its best. There are several such tasks. For example, spark plugs must be replaced when they burn out or become fouled; the propeller must be replaced if it has been damaged by an underwater obstacle; water must be added to the battery when it is low, or perhaps the battery needs to be charged. In addition, the carburetor will need adjustment from time to time; the engine occasionally will have to be removed and then remounted and adjusted to the correct angle; the steering linkage will have to be adjusted; the engine will have to be connected to the throttle and shift controls, the fuel tank, and the battery. If you plan to have someone else perform these and other routine tasks, perhaps you should rethink your decision to buy a boat. Renting (chartering) may be the best approach for you.

Figure 35. Spark plugs must be clean and properly gapped. Check them periodically to assure trouble-free performance. (*Photo courtesy of Kiekhaefer Mercury.*)

PREVENTIVE MAINTENANCE

It's one thing to decide to carry out preventive maintenance and another to actually do it. Like the proverbial road to hell, preventive maintenance country is littered with unfulfilled good intentions. There is a way, however, to avoid this trap. The trick is to systematize your approach and then to stick religiously to your system. What follows has proved to be useful to many outboarders. It may do the trick for you too.

First, thoroughly familiarize yourself with the owner's manual supplied with your engine. It will include such information as starting procedures, recommended type of fuel, recommended fuel-oil mixture, recommended spark plugs and gap settings, adjustments you the owner must make to keep the engine in peak running order, routine maintenance procedures, and so on. Consider this booklet your bible, and faithfully follow its suggestions. After all, the manufacturer of your engine wants your good will.

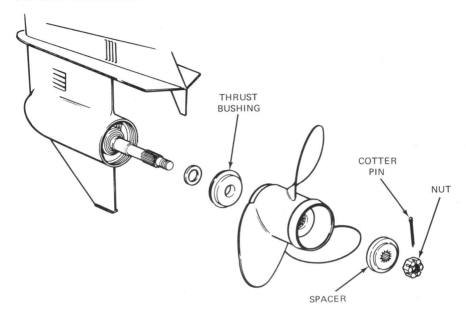

Figure 36. Exploded view of the propeller, propeller shaft, and related parts from a 50-hp outboard engine. The shaft should be cleaned and greased periodically. (*Art courtesy of Johnson Motors.*)

In particular, he wants your business when you replace the engine or move up to a larger engine. It is therefore in his best interest to give you sound and useful advice.

It isn't possible, nor would it be worth while to duplicate here all of the information found in a typical owner's manual. This you should master. What we will do here instead is lay out a systematic scheme for engine maintenance. The details of each maintenance procedure can then be looked up in the owner's manual. Incidentally, most outboard manufacturers supply service manuals also. These are much more comprehensive and detailed than owner's manuals. If you have a mechanical turn of mind, you'll probably find one of these booklets most interesting and useful.

Preventive maintenance procedures quite naturally fall into two groups: those you perform periodically throughout the boating season and those you perform each time you go out. It is suggested that boatmen in northern coastal waters perform the periodic procedures about once a month; those on inland and southern waters can carry out these procedures about once every two months. Here are the periodic checks:

Pull the propeller and clean and grease the shaft. A strip of sandpaper is useful for removing any rust or corrosion that has built up on the shaft. Also check the shaft to see if it wobbles. Any looseness detected may be a sign of bearing trouble.

While you're working on the lower unit, pull the inspection plug and check the grease level. In addition, examine the condition of the lubricant. If it is dirty or a dull gray in color, drain it out and replace with new lubricant. Be sure, however, to use the lubricant recommended by the manufacturer.

Go over the entire steering rig and grease every moving part. Pay particular attention to the swivel bracket on the engine, but don't overlook other moving parts. If your steering system uses cables and pulleys, inspect the cables for cracks in the plastic coating. Cracks mean water leakage; eventually the steel cable inside the plastic will be eaten away.

With regard to the electrical system, first examine the high-tension leads. If there are any cracks or breaks in the insulation, a spark can jump to the block from the cable and short out the engine. These breaks, incidentally, are easily repaired with electricians' tape. Check your battery for water level and charge, and don't overlook the cable connections. The cables should be removed and the terminals cleared of corrosion. Then, after reassembly, the fittings should be lightly coated with grease.

Move now to the powerhead, and grease all control linkages and moving parts. These include the shift link, throttle and choke controls, and so on. Be sure also to keep the powerhead clean. Wipe it down with a cloth, and dig out any greasy debris that may have accumulated in tight corners. The single most important advantage to a clean powerhead is that certain troubles, such as leaky gaskets, show up more readily on a clean engine.

Another important procedure is cleaning the fuel filter. Your owner's manual will tell you how. If the filter should seem excessively dirty, replace it.

Finally, remove and check the spark plugs. They may need cleaning and regapping. If the plugs are very badly fouled, or if the electrodes are deeply eaten away, it is much wiser to replace them. In addition, always keep a spare set of plugs on board, but be sure to keep them in an airtight container. They won't be very useful if they're covered with rust when you need them most.

Now let's consider the routine and simple maintenance checks you should make each time you go out in your boat. Try to make these as

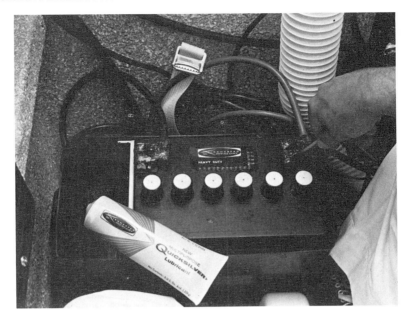

Figure 37. Engine failure is often the result of corroded battery cable connections. Clean the terminals and cover lightly with grease periodically. (*Photo courtesy of Kiekhaefer Mercury.*)

automatic as you can. They will eliminate worry from your boating as well as contribute to your enjoyment while afloat.

First, go over the entire steering system. Be sure all parts are in good condition and working order. Next, check the fuel lines and connections. Look for cracks and leaks, and repair if needed. Make sure the fuel line is plugged into the engine properly. The fitting may look right, but in fact it may not be locked in place. A sailor I know once had to sail his boat into a crowded marina, a difficult job at best, because of an engine failure that turned out to be an improperly seated fuel line connector. When he finally got to it, he corrected the trouble by giving the fitting a gentle push. It locked in place immediately, and the engine started right up.

Take a moment to examine your propeller. Look for nicks or gouges in the blades, and have these repaired if they have gone beyond the minor stage. Quickly examine all controls and linkages. Make sure all are in operating condition, but check for excessive play or vibration also. In use it is not uncommon for various parts to loosen up. Most of these problems, however, are easily corrected on the spot.

When you come in from an outing, fill your fuel tanks before going home. This will prevent the accumulation of condensed moisture in the tanks, and also get you off to a good start on your next trip. Don't overlook the need to clean your engine. Wash it down to get rid of any grime or salt that may have accumulated, and then wipe it down with an oily rag. It is important to clear the engine of unused fuel at the end of a trip. To do this, disconnect the fuel hose and allow the engine to run until all the fuel in the carburetor has been used up. This helps to keep the carburetor and fuel lines free of gummy deposits, and of course eliminates fuel spillage when the engine is being carried about.

In summary, each time you go out you should inspect the steering system, fuel lines and connections, propeller, and controls and linkages. Then, when you come in, top off the fuel tanks and clean the engine. Couple these very simple precautionary chores with the periodic maintenance described previously, and you will have covered most of what it takes to guarantee trouble-free pleasure on the water.

TROUBLE-SHOOTING

Preventive maintenance is the key to trouble-free boating. Sometimes, however, despite preventive maintenance, breakdowns do occur. Fortunately, given reasonable care, engine failures are extremely rare. Unfortunately, they always seem to happen when professional help is least available. There are no mechanics or service stations two miles offshore. For this reason every outboard owner should understand and be able to put into practice some simple principles of trouble-shooting.

The key again is a systematic approach. For the most part, engine failure can be traced to either (1) the *ignition system* or (2) the *fuel system*. A healthy, timed spark must be delivered to an adequate fuel-air charge in the cylinder.

Your first task is to determine which of these systems is at fault. Then, having established the area of trouble, you can attempt to pinpoint the exact difficulty. Begin by checking fuel delivery. Disconnect the fuel hose from the engine. Then, after aiming the fitting overboard, press a sharp pointed object against the spring-loaded valve. If fuel squirts out of the fitting, you can be sure that it is getting to the engine. If no fuel squirts out, your problem is in the fuel delivery system.

Check for spark if fuel delivery seems satisfactory. First pull the spark plug lead from one of the plugs and hold its end about one-quarter inch away from an unpainted part of the engine. Now turn the engine over either manually or with the electric start. The ignition key must be turned on. A hot, fat, blue spark should jump between the lead and the engine. No spark at all tells you that the trouble is in the ignition system.

TABLE I

TROUBLE-SHOOTING OUTBOARD ENGINES

TROUBLE	POSSIBLE CAUSE
Engine will not start, or is difficult to start.	Fuel tank vent closed. Fuel lines pinched. Engine not primed. Carburetor adjustments too lean. Engine not being choked. Improper fuel-oil mixture. Battery low, or connections bad. Spark plugs fouled or improperly gapped. Condensation on ignition system wiring.
Engine overheats.	Engine mounted too high; too little water entering cooling system. Clogged water inlet or outlet. Leaking water lines.
Engine spits, coughs, or slows.	Carburetor improperly adjusted. Fuel filter dirty. Spark plugs fouled. Kinked fuel line.
Engine seems to run well, but then slows down and stops.	Fuel pump or carburetor dirty. Insufficient lubrication. Not enough oil in gasoline. Propeller fouled. Fuel lines dirty.
Engine knocks excessively.	Too much or too little oil in gasoline.

TABLE I (cont'd.)

TROUBLE	POSSIBLE CAUSE
Engine stops suddenly.	You're out of gas!
	No oil in gasoline.
	No lubricant in lower unit gear casing.
Engine running, but boat not moving well.	Propeller fouled.
	Engine not deep enough in water.
	Wrong engine tilt.
	Propeller shear pin broken.
Excessive vibration.	Improper carburetor adjustment.
	Propeller damaged, bent, or fouled.
	Spark plug not firing.
	Transom clamp screw(s) loose.

If you've been caring for your engine, the spark plugs should be clean and properly gapped. Nevertheless, even if you get a good spark from the lead it is probably wise to check the plugs for spark also. Remove a plug, replace the lead, and hold the plug base against an unpainted part of the engine. You should see the spark jump across the spark plug gap when the engine is turned over. No spark or a weak spark indicates a defective spark plug. It may be fouled or perhaps even cracked.

When making either of these spark tests, do not touch any metal parts. Hold both the spark plug lead and the plug itself by the insulated portion. If you touch any metal part during the test a painful shock may result.

Having isolated the system that is at fault, the next step is to determine the precise source of the difficulty. The procedures will be limited here, however, to those corrective measures that the average operator can carry out. Anything more serious should be handled by a trained mechanic. Refer to Table I, which lists the most common engine problems and their causes. In most cases, the remedies are obvious, although you may want to refer to your owner's manual for detailed instructions.

FUELING SAFETY

It is a fact that the majority of gasoline explosions and fires on boats occur just after a refueling stop. Gasoline vapor trapped in the interior of the boat is usually the culprit. It is a fact also that these accidents are usually the result of carelessness, of a blatant disregard for the basic rules of fueling safety. From the safety standpoint, no boating activity is as critical as refueling. It should be thought of as a ritual ceremony, with a prescribed sequence of steps. There should never be any deviation, however small, from this sequence of steps.

As you are about to discover, refueling a boat with gasoline is quite a different matter from "gassing up" your car. This difference is largely the result of two factors: (1) gasoline vapor is heavier than air, and sinks through air to the lowest cavity available; (2) boat hulls are hollow cavities that provide numerous natural traps for gasoline vapor.

Gasoline is a highly volatile substance, as anyone standing near a gasoline nozzle can attest. But this is not the only source of gasoline vapor. During a fueling stop it rushes out of the fuel tank as liquid gasoline enters the tank and begins to fill it up. In essence, as the tank fills with liquid, the vapor above the liquid is forced out through the filling pipe. The escaping vapor flows downward; if there is an opening to the interior of a boat's hull, the vapor will find its way through this opening.

Once inside the boat, the gasoline vapor mixes with air to form a potentially explosive combination. Any spark or flame can then trigger an explosion or fire. The flame of a match, or a hot spark from a cigar, cigarette, or pipe will do the job. Or a spark from some part of the boat's electrical system may be guilty. Sparks can come from switches and automatically started motors such as those on bilge pumps, refrigerators, and air conditioners. The basic principles of fueling safety are therefore these: (1) prevent all gasoline vapors from entering the interior of a boat's hull and (2) eliminate open flames and the possibility of sparks until the entire boat has been completely ventilated *after* refueling. These goals are best achieved by close adherence to the following procedures.

If your outboard rig uses a portable gasoline tank, always remove it from the boat for refueling. This procedure applies to the dockside refueling stop, where the temptation is very great to take the fuel hose into the boat. Resist this impulse, and make the effort to disconnect the fuel tank from the engine and carry it onto the dock for refilling. This simple precaution should exclude all gasoline vapors from the interior of your boat's hull.

Many of today's outboard-powered boats carry built-in fuel tanks. The advantages to this arrangement are obvious, but refueling must be done with extreme care. This is where the ritual ceremony mentioned earlier comes in. Follow the sequence outlined here and you should stay free of explosion hazards.

- 1. Before reaching the fuel dock, try to determine how much fuel your tanks will hold. Then instruct the attendant to fill the tanks to no more than 90 per cent of the total tank capacity. This will provide space for thermal expansion of the gasoline.

- 2. After securely tying up at the dock, tightly close all hatches and doors, including all interior doors, and all ports and windows.

- 3. Stop all engines.

- 4. Make sure there are no open flames anywhere on the boat or on the dock near the fuel pump and boat. The rule here is *absolutely no smoking*.

- 5. Cut off *all* electrical power at the main battery switch to all lights, motors, and other electrical equipment.

- 6. Now remove the cap from the fuel tank filling pipe. Insist on two things when the attendant is filling the tank: first, that he keep the tip of the nozzle inside the filling pipe until the quantity of fuel ordered has been delivered, and second, that he operate the nozzle by hand pressure. Latch-type nozzles are prohibited, for they spill gasoline when they turn off. Equally important, make sure the hose nozzle remains in contact with the edge of the filling pipe to prevent a possible static spark.

- 7. When the desired quantity of gasoline has been delivered, the hose nozzle should be closed, drained, and then withdrawn from the filling pipe. Replace the cap immediately and tighten down. Flush away with water any gasoline that has been spilled.

- 8. *Do not relax.* Despite your sigh of relief and that feeling that the worst is over with, it is not! The most critical part of the entire operation is just beginning. The engines must not be started and the electric power must not be turned on until the entire boat has been ventilated for at least five minutes. Open all ports, windows, hatches, and doors. Turn on the fireproof bilge blowers if these are installed on your boat.

- 9. Check all compartments for the odor of gasoline vapors. Once you are sure there is no gasoline vapor on board, you can turn on the electric power, start the engines, and permit smoking.

These fire-prevention measures may seem drastic. If you've ever seen an explosion afloat or talked to someone who has survived such an accident, however, you will know how realistic and necessary they are. Any refueling sequence less thorough than this one openly courts disaster. The choice is clearly yours to make.

All two-cycle outboard engines require that the lubricating oil be mixed with the gasoline. The key word here is *mixed*. If the oil is simply dumped in the bottom of the fuel tank and the gasoline added, the chances are that the two components will not mix thoroughly. Complete mixing, however, is vital to proper engine performance. In fact, it is more important than getting the exact oil-gasoline ratio.

The best way to guarantee complete mixing is to blend by shaking in the tank equal volumes of oil and gasoline prior to adding the remaining fuel. Once this starting blend has been completely mixed, the remaining gasoline can be added. If this procedure is followed, a properly mixed fuel should result.

THE DUMPED ENGINE

Few accidents on the water are as shattering as losing the engine overboard. Any good skipper shudders at the mere thought of this one, and with good reason. Water is the archenemy of the moving parts and internal chambers of an engine. There are bad, and there are very bad dump jobs. Losing your engine in salt water is worse than losing it in fresh water. And dropping a running engine overboard is the worst that can possibly happen. Before the engine quits it will suck in water and silt and greatly increase the possibility of serious damage.

The key to handling an engine that has been immersed is quick action *after* it has been removed from the water. Be less concerned about getting it out of the water quickly. Once it is out, however, the oxygen of the air will begin at once to corrode internal metal surfaces that have been exposed to water during the dunking.

Do not wait! As little as an extra hour may prove to be very costly. As quickly as possible, take the engine to a competent outboard mechanic and tell him what happened. He may elect to try to start the engine to restore internal lubrication, or he may tear it down at once. In any event, he is best qualified to take whatever action is needed to restore the engine to working order.

STORING THE ENGINE

Storing an outboard engine between trips during the boating season is a simple task, as pointed out earlier. The engine is run until all the fuel in the carburetor has been used up. Then, if the engine is removed from the boat, it is held upright until the cooling system has drained completely.

Winter storage and storage for more than just a few days during the season require more elaborate procedures. These are well within the capabilities of the average outboarder, however, and if followed carefully can save the cost of in-shop storage and servicing. What follows is the typical procedure for most outboards. Check your owner's manual for any deviations.

- 1. The last time you run the engine, stop it by choking. This will put a layer of the oil-fuel mixture on the interior surfaces.
- 2. Be sure all water has been drained out of the cooling system.
- 3. Remove and clean the fuel filter bowl on the fuel pump.
- 4. Lubricate the engine as specified by your owner's manual; include replacement of the lower unit lubricant if the manuel recommends it.
- 5. Remove the spark plugs and pour several tablespoonfuls of two-cycle oil into the cylinders. Distribute the oil by pulling the starter cord several times, and then replace the plugs finger tight.
- 6. Store the engine in an upright position in a dry place. You can build a simple rack or purchase a stand at a reasonable price.

Note also that the gasoline tank should be emptied. Gasoline should not be stored for long periods of time.

Putting your engine back in running shape is a simple task. Remove the plugs first and then expel the excess oil in the cylinders by pulling the starter cord. Check the plugs and clean and regap them or replace them if necessary. Your engine should now be ready to go.

6. MARLINSPIKE SEAMANSHIP

A MARLINSPIKE IS A POINTED wood or steel wedge used to open strands of rope and wire for splicing. And splicing, of course, is one of the important ways to join two pieces of rope or wire. Needless to say, many different types of objects are fastened together on a boat. In hundreds of years, the use of rope on board a boat has come to be known as marlinspike seamanship. It's important that you learn some of these fundamentals, for without them you will find handling a boat a difficult task. The skills of marlinspike seamanship require practice. Many boatmen find practicing knots and splices during the winter a worthwhile pastime. It helps to keep one's skills in top shape and also to make the long winter easier to get through.

What is rope? In all ropes that are not braided, *fibers* are twisted to the right to form *yarns,* yarns are twisted to the left to form *strands,* and strands are twisted to the right to form *ropes.* Such ropes are said to be laid right-handed. They must be coiled clockwise to avoid kinks and twists. Try it for yourself. Coil a piece of rope clockwise and counterclockwise. What happens when you pull rope off the coil in each instance?

Of the ropes in general use on boats today, two are of plant origin and two are synthetic. Manila and sisal are the natural-fiber ropes, and nylon and Dacron are the synthetics. There are great advantages to nylon and Dacron ropes, which explains why you see them in use on so many boats. They are more costly than Manila or sisal, but their advantages far outweigh the additional cost.

Nylon rope has a very high elasticity and great strength for its weight.

Thus it is very useful for anchor, mooring, and docking lines, as well as for towing lines. Its elasticity provides a built-in spring that absorbs many of the jolts and sharp tugs a boat encounters at anchor or tied up to a dock. Its great strength, of course, allows the use of a much lighter and less bulky line for most jobs. In addition, nylon fiber is waterproof and highly resistant to rot. It can be stowed away while still wet, an impossibility with Manila or sisal, both of which are subject to rot.

Handle nylon rope that is under tension with great respect. Its elasticity makes it a threat to the safety of the unwary. A stretched nylon tow line can tear free and snap back with alarming suddenness and great force. It pays to stand clear of any nylon tow line.

Dacron rope has less strength than nylon, but it has the advantage of a very low elasticity. Thus it finds use in halyards and sheet lines on sailboats, where stretching is undesirable. Dacron rope is very easy to work, being soft, pliable, and easy on the hands.

KNOTS, HITCHES, AND BENDS

Up to this point we have been talking about rope. The boatman uses rope for many things, but he generally refers to it as *line* when it is in use on board a boat. Line may be fastened to itself, to another line, or to some object. This is where *knots, hitches,* and *bends* come in. Knots are used to bind objects together or to secure a bundle or package. A hitch is used to secure a line to another object, and a bend joins two line ends to each other. You should know certain knots, hitches, and bends before venturing out by yourself on a boat. There are few things more embarrassing than the mishap that sometimes occurs because a knot, hitch, or bend is improperly tied.

Of the knots, three are an absolute must. These are the *reef* (or square) knot, the *figure-eight* knot, and the *bowline*. Figure 38 shows how these knots are tied. The square knot serves many purposes: lashing objects to the deck, tying in battens, reefing, fastening down covers on a sailboat, and so on. Be careful, though, to tie the square knot correctly. The incorrect version, the *granny* knot, slips easily. In addition, never use the square knot as a bend—that is, to tie two ropes together. Almost certainly the knot will slip.

The figure eight is useful as a *stopper* knot. Tie it into the free end of lines to prevent them from running out through blocks or fairleads should

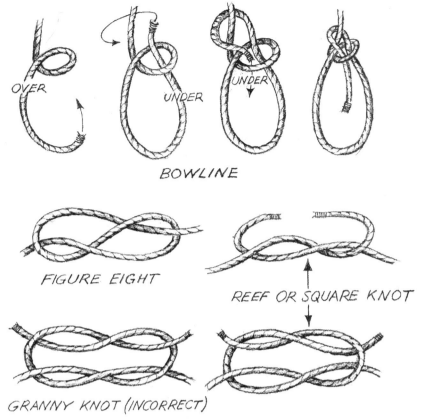

OVER

UNDER

UNDER

BOWLINE

FIGURE EIGHT

REEF OR SQUARE KNOT

GRANNY KNOT (INCORRECT)

Figure 38. Knots bind objects together, or secure a package. These knots (with the exception of the "granny") are essential to the skilled boatman.

the line get away from you. Avoid the simple overhand knot, though. It tends to jam, and it is difficult to untie.

The bowline is the single most important knot available to the boatman. It is used to fasten a line to an object or to put a loop at the end of a line. Its most important advantage is that it will never slip, nor will it ever jam. A properly tied bowline is very simple to release once the tension has been taken off. The drawing in Figure 38 shows how to tie a bowline. The first step is to make a small loop in the line, leaving enough line free to make a large loop of the desired size. The free end is then passed through the small loop as shown, under the standing part, and back through the small loop. You should learn how to tie a bowline blindfolded. The day (or night) may come when you will be glad you did.

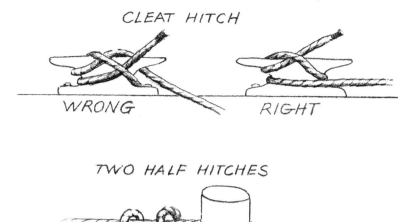

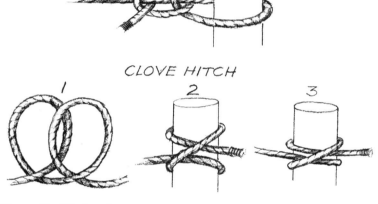

Figure 39. Hitches fasten a line to an object. When tying up, be sure to use the proper hitch, and be doubly sure it is properly tied.

Hitches, as mentioned, are used to secure a line to an object. For example, you might wish to fasten a line to a pile, a bitt, a spar, or a ring. Often, for strictly temporary tying up, a *clove hitch* is used to fasten a docking line to a pile. Under no circumstances, however, should a clove hitch be regarded as secure or permanent. A clove hitch pulls out quite easily if it is subjected to tugs and pulls from different directions.

A more secure hitch is the familiar *two half hitches*. More people than not tie two half hitches without realizing exactly what they are doing. This is a useful and important hitch. It is often used by itself, but it also finds use as a safety hitch. For example, the clove hitch can be made more secure by half-hitching the line's end to its standing part.

FISHERMAN'S BEND

SHEET BEND

DOUBLE SHEET BEND

Figure 40. Bends fasten two line ends to each other. The fisherman's "bend"—really a hitch—is a useful way to fasten anchor line to the anchor ring.

No boatman can get by without knowing how to fasten a line to a cleat. Thus the *cleat hitch* must be learned—and correctly. A quick look at how a boatman ties his cleat hitches will tell you more about his ability as a seaman than any other skill. Look closely the next time you wander around a marina. Some of the "rat's nests" passing for cleat hitches are appalling. Moreover, they are apt to pull out. It's *how* you fasten a line to a cleat, not how many turns you wrap on, that counts.

Many inexperienced boatmen make the mistake of using the wrong kind of fastening to attach two line ends to each other. The correct fastening is the *sheet bend*. Figure 40 shows two types of sheet bend: the double sheet bend, used for fastening light line to heavy line, and the ordinary sheet bend, used to connect lines with nearly the same diameter. The other fastening shown—the *fisherman's bend*—is not really a bend. It is a hitch. Boatmen insist on calling it a bend, however, so we will also.

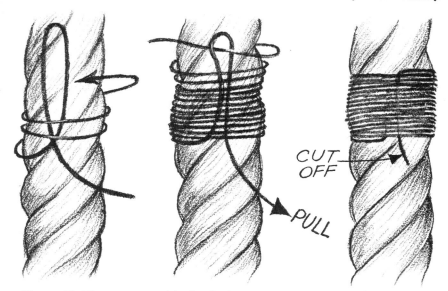

Figure 41. The common whipping is the easiest to apply, although it does not stand up as well as the more elaborate cord whippings.

The fisherman's bend is used to fasten the anchor line to the ring or shackle of your anchor. It is a quick, easy, and secure substitute for an eye splice made around a thimble. The two turns of the fisherman's bend around the ring or shackle will wear, however, so the bend should be inspected and retied occasionally.

WHIPPING

Another clue to the seamanship ability of a boatman is the condition of the ends of his lines. If his lines are unraveling at their ends, or if they have bulky knots tied into the ends to prevent unraveling, you can be sure of questionable seamanship skills. The lines of a good seaman are neatly and properly whipped.

There are several ways to whip a line end in this day of synthetic materials. With the introduction of waterproof tapes, for example, some boatmen have taken to using tape whipping. This is a good temporary whipping, but it should be replaced with something more permanent, for sooner or later the tape slips off. Another modern whipping consists of a plastic sleeve slightly larger in diameter than the line to be whipped. The sleeve is slipped into place and then heated with a match or lighter flame. The plastic shrinks up tight after cooling. A useful trick when nylon or Dacron line is being whipped is burning the end of the line with a flame. The synthetic melts and fuses, forming a small knob of greater diameter at the end of the line. This prevents unraveling and holds the whipping in place.

The more traditional whipping consists of some form of light, strong cord wrapped around the end of the line. Sailmakers' thread, waxed sail twine, or even stout nylon thread may be used. Figure 41 shows the easiest of the traditional whippings, the common whipping. Other whippings are more difficult to do, but last longer than common whipping.

SPLICES

A final skill with rope required of all boatmen is the art of splicing. There are many different types of splices for the dedicated seaman to learn. For our purposes, however, two will suffice. These are the *eye splice,* for forming a permanent loop, and the *short splice,* for permanently joining two pieces of line of equal diameter. The short splice is quite easy, but it will not pass through a block or fairlead because it doubles the diameter of the line. If the line must pass through a block, the long splice must be used.

Figure 42 shows how an eye splice is made. The first step is to unwind three strands to a length of about eight inches. Tightly tape the line at the base of the unwound portion, and also tape the ends of the strands. In an eye splice, the first series of tucks is the most difficult, so follow the drawing carefully. First, push the middle strand A under one of the strands on the standing part. Next, pass B over the strand that A went under and tuck it under the next strand to the left. Note that all tucks go from right to left. Finally, turn the splice over and tuck C from right to left under the strand that lies between A and B. Now pull the tucks tight and start the next series of tucks. From this point on, A, B, and C each go over their next strand and under the following strand. For Manila line, three to four tucks is enough. For nylon line you should put in six or seven tucks to compensate for the slipperiness of the material. Remove the tape from the loop before smoothing out the splice.

The approach to the short splice is the same as in the eye splice—all

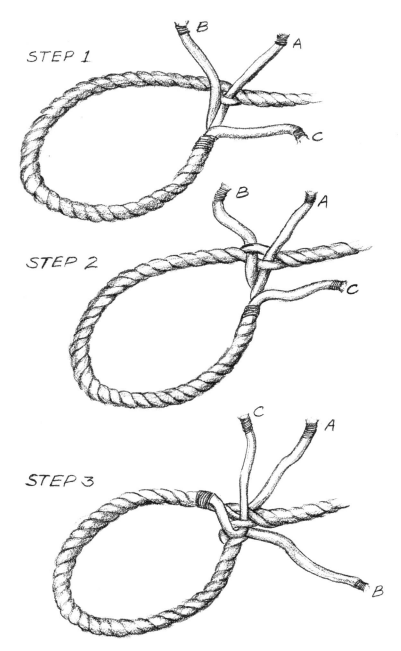

Figure 42. All boatmen should be able to make an eye splice, for numerous lines aboard a boat call for the neatly looped end of an eye splice.

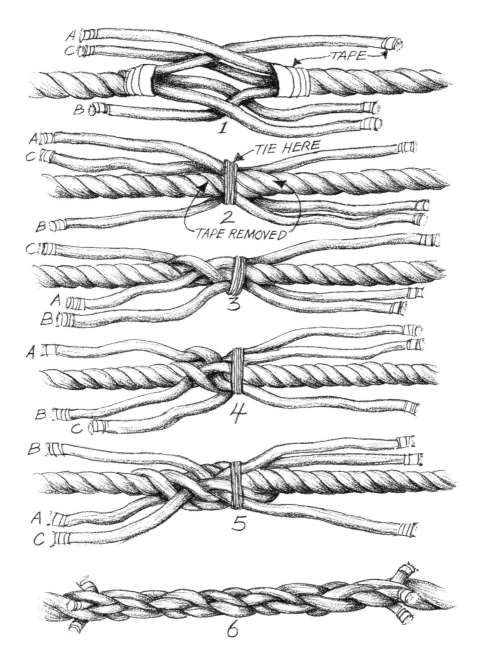

Figure 43. The short splice permanently joins two line ends together. It doubles the volume of the line, however, and will not pass easily through a block or fairlead.

tucks go over one and under one from right to left against the lay of the strands. See Figure 43. First, tape each piece of line about eight inches from the ends and at the end of each of the strands. Next, run the two pieces of line together as shown in steps 1 and 2, and tie them together tightly where they join. The tapes can now be removed. Make your first tuck as shown in step 3, going from right to left with strand A. Then rotate the splice and make the next tuck with strand B, as shown in step 4. Step 5 shows the third and last tuck, using strand C. Now continue on in turn, and make two additional series of tucks. This completes half the splice.

The other half of the splice is started by turning the line around in your lap. Complete three tucks with each strand, and pound and roll the splice on a hard surface to evenly distribute the strands and smooth out the splice. Both the short splice and the eye splice are completed by cutting away the excess and then whipping the end of each strand.

7. UNDER WAY!

WELL, THERE IT IS: your brand-new (to you, anyway) outboard boat, fully outfitted and raring to go. All you have to do is jump in, start the engine, and take off. Or do you? Pause a moment to think this one over. You're reading this book because you want to learn about boating before actually heading out by yourself. And as you are discovering, there's plenty to learn. It stands to reason, then, that you have little or no experience handling a fast and powerful boat. Very probably, in fact, other than a trial run or two in the boat lying there, outboarding is to you a brand-new sport. What you make of it depends upon what you put into it. Reading this book is a good start. It shows that you care about seamanship, safety, courtesy afloat, and the many other important aspects of boating.

This chapter concerns itself with handling an outboard afloat. (Later we'll discuss trailering your boat.) Starting at the beginning, we'll cover how to get yourself and your gear aboard, how to cast off and leave a dock, how to approach a mooring and a dock, how to beach your boat, what to look for when boating on a river, and finally, how to tie up correctly and secure the boat. In addition, we'll discuss the importance of proper trim and its effect on the stability of your boat, as well as the dangers of overloading. Other problems, such as boating under rough conditions, learning to read the weather, and basic piloting will be taken up in later chapters.

GETTING STARTED

As we said, there it is, tied up to the dock as pretty as a picture, just waiting to take off. Your first impulse, of course, is to jump aboard and get started. Don't, however, jump into a small boat! You may capsize it, damage it, or even hurt yourself. Also, don't board a small boat by stepping on the gunwale. Again, the danger is that the boat may capsize. Instead, go aboard by stepping carefully to as near the center of the boat as possible. This will keep the boat balanced until all passengers and gear are aboard.

With respect to gear—life preservers, the lunch box, gasoline tank, portable icebox, extra warm clothing, and so on—wait until you are in the boat before taking it aboard. The best way is to have someone on the dock hand you the gear before coming aboard himself.

With all hands and all gear aboard and settled, you are ready to start the engine and go—*after* running through the following safety checklist. This and other checklists to be introduced later will help you reduce the problem of maintaining safety standards to an easily managed routine. Don't skip these routine checkoffs—it's amazing what can be overlooked or forgotten when a routine is not followed. Here are the questions. You need the answers to get under way.

- Are there enough life preservers on board?
- How about the rest of the required safety equipment? Is it all in functioning order?
- Do all passengers know where the life preservers and other safety equipment are stored?
- Is the boat overloaded with either people or gear?
- Are passengers and gear distributed so that the boat is in good trim?
- Is the bilge free of excess water and gasoline and oil?
- Have you checked the bilge for dangerous fumes?
- Have you sufficient fuel and oil on board?
- Have you run through the engine checklist outlined in Chapter 5?
- Is your boat registration card on board?
- Have you the proper charts on board?
- Have you checked the latest weather forecast?
- Have you checked the water current, the wind direction, and sea conditions?

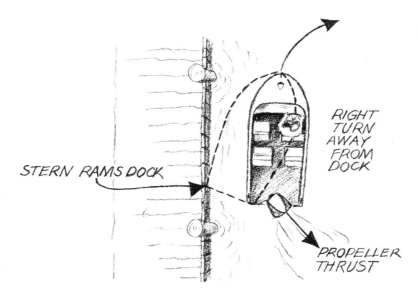

Figure 44. How not to leave a dock. When the direction of propeller thrust is changed to turn the boat away, the stern is rammed into the side of the dock.

- Is all loose gear secured?
- Is the engine warmed up and running smoothly?

With the correct answers to these questions (and any others that apply specifically to your boat) you are ready to take in or cast off the mooring lines and get under way.

LEAVING A DOCK

To pull an automobile away from the curb, you simply turn the wheel and drive the car out. Unfortunately, it isn't quite as simple to pull an outboard-powered boat away from a dock. Outboards are steered by changing the direction of the propeller's thrust. When the engine is turned to change the direction of thrust, the stern of the boat responds by swinging to the side. In a manner of speaking, the boat is steered by shifting the position of the stern until the bow points in the desired direction. Thus, if you attempt to turn a boat lying parallel to a dock and motor out, the stern will probably ram the dock. At the least this is an embarrassingly unseamanlike maneuver. At the other end of the scale, you run the risk of seriously damaging the hull.

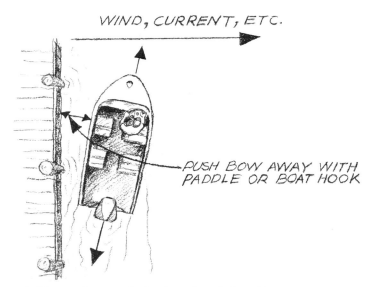

Figure 45. How to leave a dock when the wind and/or current are coming off the dock. First, push the bow out. Then motor away when there
is room ahead to clear obstacles. Propeller thrust should be dead astern.

In general, the problem of leaving a dock comes down to two basic
conditions: wind and/or current moving *away from* the dock, and wind
and/or current moving *toward* the dock.

When the wind and/or current are moving away from the dock, pulling
free is seldom a problem. In fact, the wind or current usually assists in
clearing the boat. See Figure 45. The procedure is quite straightforward.
First cast off the bow and stern lines. Then, as the boat begins to drift
free of the dock, use a boat hook or paddle to push the bow out enough to
permit you to motor away from the dock at low speed. Proceed at low
speed and with great care until you are well clear of the dock. Under the
rules of the road (see Chapter 11), a boat leaving a dock must avoid all
other craft until it is clear.

Leaving a dock is not quite as simple when the wind and/or current are
moving toward the dock. In this case, the effect is to hold the boat
against the dock, making it difficult to get clear. If the wind or current is
not very strong, you may be able to push the bow off as in the case above.
More than likely, however, this won't work, and you will be forced to
resort to a different tactic. In this case, the trick is to pull the stern clear
before going forward. See Figure 46.

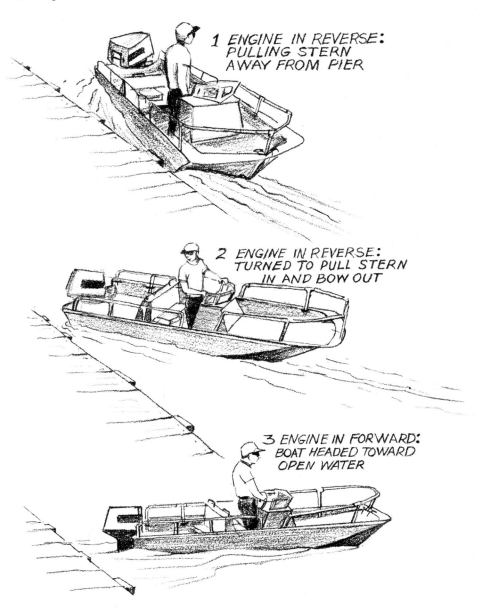

Figure 46. When the wind and/or current are moving toward a dock, it is necessary to pull the stern away first when leaving in order to get clear of the dock. If done properly, this maneuver leaves the bow pointed out from the dock with plenty of space aft.

First cast off the docking lines. Then, with the engine in reverse and turned away from the dock, pull the stern clear. Operate at the lowest speed that gives you steerageway. The next step is to turn the engine back toward the dock, leaving it in reverse. This will pull the stern in and point the bow out. If this maneuver is done correctly, the boat will end up with plenty of space aft and the bow pointed out, away from the dock. At this point shift into forward gear and motor away from the dock.

HOW DOES YOUR CRAFT HANDLE?

One of the most important things you should do with a new boat is to learn its handling characteristics thoroughly. One or two trial runs before buying don't tell you nearly enough. The only way to really master a boat is to take it out repeatedly, under a variety of conditions. With enough experience at the helm, your craft is unlikely to fool you when the going gets rough or you are operating in close quarters.

For your first outing with a new boat, plan to operate on well-protected, calm waters. Be sure you put the boat through all its paces. For example, how quickly does it respond to a turn of the wheel? Try this at several different speeds. You may be surprised at its quickness, or perhaps by an unexpected sluggishness. Find out how much distance is required to slow down from planing to idling speeds. This knowledge might someday prevent a serious injury—to yourself, a passenger, or perhaps to a water skier who has dumped in front of your boat.

Find out the low-speed turning radius of the boat for both clockwise and counterclockwise turns. It may differ. A handy way to do this is to use a buoy for a reference point. Practice turns around the buoy at various radii and speeds in both directions. See Figure 47. Keep at it until you have the feel of what the boat will do in a turn. Avoid tight, high-speed turns at all times. This maneuver is highly dangerous. In fact, it is the leading cause of capsizal, which in turn is the leading cause of fatal motorboating accidents. Fortunately, tight, high-speed turns are practically never called for under normal operating conditions. If you ever find yourself forced to turn sharply at high speeds, then you were probably traveling too fast to begin with.

All craft under way are subject to the rules of the road. These "traffic" regulations dictate how boats must maneuver to avoid collision. Often, however, it is difficult to apply the "rules" because the traffic patterns are complex and confusing. When this happens, as it often does in crowded

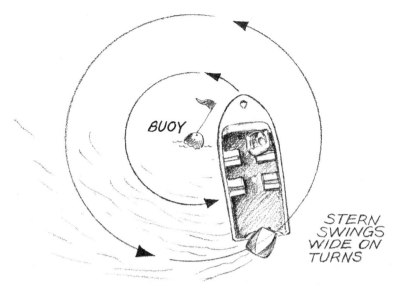

BUOY

STERN
SWINGS
WIDE ON
TURNS

Figure 47. Determine the low-speed turning characteristics of your boat by running practice turns in both directions around a buoy.

harbors and anchorages, the governing rule becomes common sense and courtesy. It is foolish, often discourteous, and sometimes dangerous to insist upon the right of way in a complex traffic situation when deviation from the rules is the common-sense thing to do. But more about the rules of the road later.

There's more to being under way than mastery of your boat's handling characteristics. The movements of other boats, both sail and power, the weather, the tide and current, the safety and comfort of your passengers or crew, and so on, must also be considered. It is the mark of a good seaman to know *what* to do *when* conditions call for action. This requires knowledge, skill, and a high degree of alertness. Use the following checklist of questions while you are underway, and you'll be ready for most eventualities.

- What is the condition of the boat's bilges? Have you taken too much water aboard? Can you smell gasoline fumes?
- Have you enough fuel?
- Are you constantly on the lookout for obstructions, be they debris in the water or boat traffic?
- Is all gear on board properly stowed away?

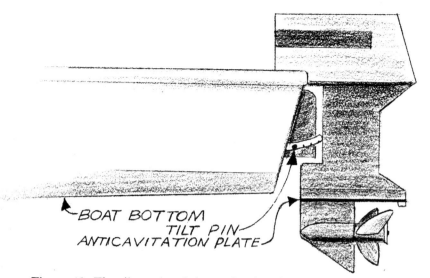

BOAT BOTTOM
TILT PIN
ANTICAVITATION PLATE

Figure 48. The tilt angle of the engine is critical to good performance. Before running trials in the water, set the angle so that the anticavitation plate is parallel to the boat's bottom.

- Are you constantly aware of the location of the nearest harbor of refuge, just in case you need it?
- Are you maintaining a weather lookout? Does this include frequent checks of the marine weather forecast, as well as visual monitoring of cloud formations and the horizon?
- Are you watching buoys to see that you stay in the proper channels? Or are you using a chart and visual signs to monitor the depth of the water?

TRIM AND OVERLOADING

To operate an outboard-powered boat at maximum efficiency, especially at planing speeds, it is necessary (1) to adjust the tilt angle of the engine correctly and (2) to distribute the boat's load evenly. The angle between the exhaust casing of the engine and the boat's transom is particularly important, for the thrust of the propeller should be parallel to the surface of the water at planing speeds. The tilt adjustment is located at the lower end of the transom bracket. See Figure 48.

WRONG! BOW DOWN

A

WRONG! BOW UP

B

RIGHT! PLANE OR EVEN KEEL

C

Figure 49. The direction of propeller thrust for a given load determines how the boat will ride. When thrust is parallel to the surface of the water the boat will achieve maximum performance.

For a given load, the angle of the propeller's thrust has a marked effect on how the boat rides. For example, with too much downward thrust the bow tends to dig in [Figure 49(A)]. If this effect is severe, the boat may swamp. Or the stern may swing around the bow, leading to a broach. With the thrust toward the surface, on the other hand, the stern of the boat tends to dig into the water [Figure 49(B)]. When this happens, the handling characteristics of the boat become highly unpredictable. The boat is difficult to control, and in extreme cases it may bounce forward like a leaping frog.

Adjust the tilt angle properly, however, and the boat will plane easily and attain its maximum rated speed [Figure 49(C)]. It will operate with the smallest possible wetted surface and produce a minimum wake. The best way to determine the proper tilt angle for a given load is to run a series of tests. First set the tilt angle so that the anticavitation plate is parallel to the boat's bottom. This can be done with the boat still on its trailer. Then use different tilt angles and evaluate the riding characteristics for each one. Try redistributing the boat's load also. With a bit of practice you will acquire a "feel" for the best angle setting.

Steering is affected also by improper propeller thrust and angle. When the thrust is parallel to the surface of the water, the blades of the propeller bite evenly into the water, both when they are ascending and when they are descending. The result is a uniform thrust, and the boat is driven directly forward. When the tilt angle is incorrect, however, the blades bite into the water unevenly on opposite sides of the propeller. The result is an uneven thrust, which causes the boat to turn away from a straight course. If this seems to be happening to your boat, check the propeller thrust angle. A small tilt adjustment may correct or minimize the problem.

Having established the correct tilt angle for the average load you intend to carry, it is now necessary to take into account how this load will be distributed within the boat. As a matter of fact, proper load distribution is essential to the determination of correct propeller thrust angle. We separated the two factors here for the sake of simplicity. In practice, they are inseparable.

Let's assume that you do your boating with two good friends, and that each of you weighs 180 pounds. We'll assume also that you normally load aboard about 100 pounds of food, drink, ice, and other gear. How do you suppose the boat will ride if all of this gear is stowed forward in the bow, and the three of you sit in the front seat? See Figure 50. That's 640

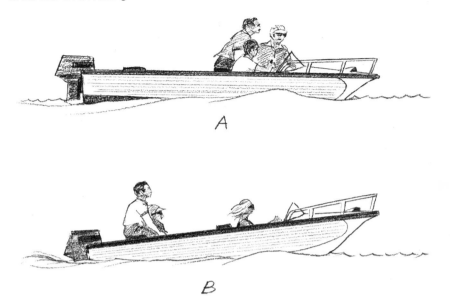

Figure 50. Load distribution is an important factor in how a boat rides. Avoid (a) loading all the weight forward and (b) loading it all aft.

pounds of man and gear loaded into the forward end of the boat. It shouldn't surprise you to find the boat noseheavy and sluggish. To correct this problem, simply redistribute the load until the boat rides properly. You might shift some of the gear; or move your two friends aft, and then take turns at the helm. This way the boat will ride properly, and everyone will share the fun.

Just as uneven distribution of load can lead to operating hazards, *over-loading* is a potentially dangerous practice also. In fact, overloading is a leading cause of boating accidents. In addition, too much weight may make it impossible to get the boat up on a plane. The boating beginner, unaware of the load limitations of his boat, often feels that it is safe to put a passenger in every seat and fill every locker with gear. Nothing could be farther from the truth. The presence of eight seats in a boat does not mean that it is safe to carry eight passengers. These are merely seating locations for the number of passengers that constitutes a safe load. For most open boats in the fifteen-to-twenty-foot range, this number will be closer to four people than to eight people.

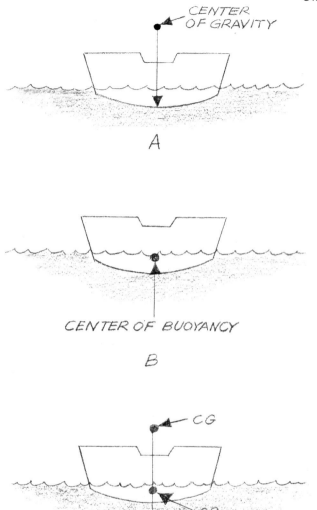

Figure 51. The relationship between center of gravity (CG) and center of buoyancy (CB) when the boat is floating on an even keel.

The load limitation of a boat is expressed in terms of total weight, including an average number of passengers for normal operating conditions. Check your boat for a BIA (Boating Industry Association) certification plate. Boats built and equipped in compliance with BIA standards carry this plate. The plate will show maximum figures for weight, number of persons, and engine horsepower for normal operating conditions. We can't emphasize too strongly that these are *maximum* figures. They must be treated as such.

Be sure also to distribute the load in your boat for lateral balance. A well-balanced, fully loaded boat should show no list to either side and should look level to the eye or just slightly down at the stern.

The hazards of overloading a boat are brought home by a tragedy that took place in the waters off Boston a few years ago. What started as a pleasant fishing trip became a disaster when three young boys drowned after their boat, an eight-foot pram, was capsized by wind and waves. The operator of the boat, the father of two of the boys, was rescued. He hung onto the overturned boat after being thrown into the water.

The deeper tragedy is that this accident need not have happened. If minimum standards of safety had been adhered to, it could have been avoided. To begin with, the boat was severely overloaded. Picture, if you will, an eight-foot pram heading out into open water with an adult male, two fourteen-year-olds, and a ten-year-old on board. When the boat capsized, it was at least a mile from the nearest land. The second tragic mistake was that no one was wearing a life jacket.

Knowledgeable boatmen will shake their heads in disbelief. An eight-foot-long pram, heavily overloaded with four people and goodness knows how much gear, heading out into open water on a windy and rough day with no one wearing a life jacket! The capsizal, unfortunately, was inevitable. Accidents will happen if basic safety rules are ignored and boats are pressed beyond their capacity. In 1970, for example, 389 of 1,418 fatal boating accidents were directly attributable to overloading. It is the responsibility of every skipper to see to it that this sort of thing is prevented.

STABILITY

If you've spent any time at all around small boats, you no doubt have heard the admonition, "Keep your weight low in the boat." There's a good reason for this. The stability of a boat depends, in general, on two factors: the hull form (see Chapter 2) and the location of the boat's *center of gravity*. The center of gravity, however, is a function of the horizontal and vertical distribution of weight within the boat. The lower the placement of the load within the boat, the lower the center of gravity and the greater the boat's stability. This is why it is unwise to stand up in a small boat to pull the engine's starter cord, or to stand erect at the bow when handling the anchor and anchor line. The resulting decrease in stability increases the boat's vulnerability to an accidental capsizal.

The center of gravity of a boat is defined as the point through which the entire weight of the boat and its load seem to pass. Put another way, if the boat could be lifted out of the water by a chain fastened at the center of gravity, the boat would remain on an even keel while suspended. As shown in Figure 51(A), when the hull is on an even keel in the water, the weight of the boat acts straight down through the center of gravity and the boat's keel.

For the boat to float, however, its weight must be opposed by an equal but upward force. This force is buoyancy. Total buoyant force, like total weight, is represented as acting through a single point. This is the *center of buoyancy* [Figure 51(B)]. The center of buoyancy is located at the geometric center of the submerged portion of the boat. For any boat floating on an even keel, the center of gravity (CG) lies directly over the center of buoyancy (CB). The weight of the boat is exactly offset by the force of buoyancy, and it floats evenly [Figure 51(C)].

When a hull rolls, however, as a result of wind, waves, or a change in course, its weight still acts vertically downward, although no longer along the line extending through the keel. The weight now acts downward along a line to the side of the keel. See Figure 52. It follows that if the center of gravity were higher, at CG', the downward force would be farther out from the centerline. As you can see, the force downward through CG' has a greater tipping effect than the force acting through CG. This is why it is important to keep the load weight as low as possible in a hull.

It is true also that when a boat rolls, the shape, or geometry, of the submerged portion changes. But if the shape of the submerged part of the hull changes, the center of buoyancy will also shift. Recall that the center of buoyancy is located at the geometric center of the submerged part of the hull. This effect is shown in Figure 52 also.

For a hull rolled to one side, the combined effects of weight (downward) and buoyancy (upward) determine if the boat will right itself or capsize. In Figure 53(A), note that the upward force exerted by buoyancy along the line CB'Z is *outside* the downward force exerted by the boat's weight along the line below CG. The dotted line CGZ is called the *righting arm;* this "arm" acts in the same manner as a crowbar, pivoted at the point CG. The buoyant force CB' pushing upward at the end of the crowbar clearly has a much stronger effect than the opposing downward force of the boat's weight. This is called *positive stability.*

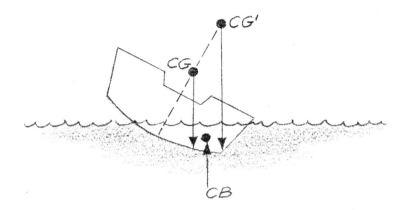

Figure 52. The higher the center of gravity the greater the tipping effect of the weight of the boat and its load.

If the center of gravity CG is high enough, however, the center of buoyancy CB' cannot move out far enough during a roll to offset the capsizing effect of weight. This is shown in Figure 53(B). Here there is no stability, and the downward effect of weight through the very high center of gravity will capsize the boat. The moral of the story? Keep the weight you take on board reasonably low, especially in rough weather.

The effect of water in the bilges bears special mention. In most pleasure boats this trapped water is free to shift from side to side as the boat rolls. This is dangerous, however, for as the water shifts to the low side of a rolling boat, it redistributes weight to that side. This results in a shift of the center of gravity toward the low side, and effectively *reduces* the righting arm of buoyancy. Given sufficient water in the bilges, it can exert enough tipping force during a roll to capsize the boat.

In general, a boat with a low center of gravity is said to be *stiff*—such craft right themselves readily. The opposite, when the center of gravity is high, is called *tenderness*. The rolls of a tender craft are long and slow. Fortunately, most small pleasure boats are on the stiff side. You can help to keep it that way by loading the boat so that the center of gravity remains low.

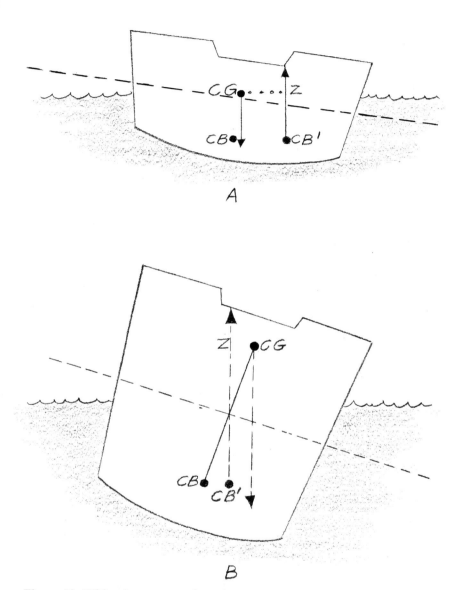

Figure 53. With a low center of gravity (A) the boat is said to have positive stability. When the center of gravity is high enough, however, the
tipping effect of the weight overcomes the righting effect of buoyancy,
and the boat capsizes (B).

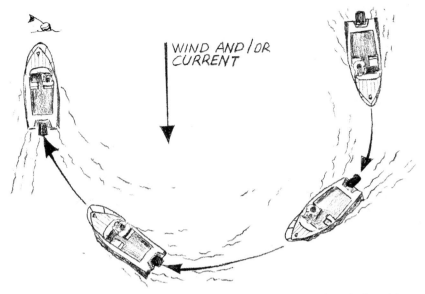

Figure 54. How to approach a mooring. Round up into the wind and/or current and bring the boat to a dead halt just as the bow reaches the mooring float.

APPROACHING A MOORING

A great many boats are stored on moorings between outings. A mooring is simply a large, permanently placed anchor from which chain and line lead to a floating buoy. Depending upon the area available, there may be plenty of room or very little room for maneuvering between boats tied up to moorings. As a small-boat skipper, you will no doubt use just your own mooring. Thus, once you get accustomed to it, you should have little or no trouble. Cruising boat skippers, on the other hand, often "borrow" moorings in strange ports, and must be able to adapt to varying conditions.

The basic tactic in approaching and picking up a mooring is quite simple. The idea is to approach the mooring buoy slowly, with the bow headed into the wind or current, whichever is strongest. A quick look around at moored boats when you are entering the harbor will tell you at once whether the wind or the current is prevailing. Of course, if the wind and current are both moving in the same direction, there is no problem. The boat is simply headed into both.

As Figure 54 shows, the final approach to the mooring consists of turning up into the wind or current and bringing the boat to a complete stop just as the bow reaches the mooring float. A member of the crew should be forward to pick the mooring pennant, buoy, and mooring eye out of the water. On boats with a low freeboard, this is easily done by hand. On larger boats a boat hook will be needed to snag the buoy.

It is often impossible for the helmsman to see the mooring buoy during the last few feet of the approach. When this happens, the crew member forward should hand signal or call back instructions to turn either to port or starboard. When the mooring eye is finally aboard and in place over the bow cleat, the skipper should briefly run the engine in reverse to stop any forward motion remaining.

Leaving a mooring requires the opposite tactic. First the eye, buoy, and pennant are dropped overboard. The boat is then backed down away from the mooring until the helmsman has a clear view of the buoy in the water. Only after he sees the buoy clearly should he go forward slowly, steering a course away from the floating gear. Carelessly running over a mooring should be avoided at all cost. It can take hours to clear a fouled propeller.

APPROACHING A DOCK

Approaching a dock is not a difficult maneuver if the wind and current are taken into account. Shallow-draft outboard boats moving at low speeds are rather easily blown about by even modest breezes. As a result, it is wise to practice coming into a dock under varying wind conditions. This wind effect can be very annoying. I've seen more than one infuriated and frustrated outboard skipper repeatedly blown off course as he attempted to approach a dock or back into a slip.

In general, there are just two conditions to be concerned with. These are wind and/or current moving toward the dock, and wind and/or current moving away from the dock. If you have a choice, avoid approaching a dock from the windward side. Given the vulnerability to wind of shallow-draft outboards, you run the risk of having the boat slammed into the dock and damaged. This is especially true if the wind is strong.

If you have no choice, however, handle the situation as shown in Figure 55. First put out fenders. Then slowly move in, as nearly parallel to the dock as possible. If you are moving slowly enough, simply put the

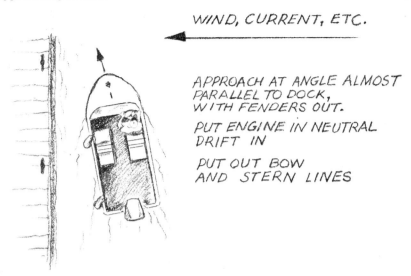

WIND, CURRENT, ETC.

APPROACH AT ANGLE ALMOST
PARALLEL TO DOCK,
WITH FENDERS OUT.

PUT ENGINE IN NEUTRAL
DRIFT IN

PUT OUT BOW
AND STERN LINES

Figure 55. How to approach a dock with the wind and/or current moving toward the dock.

engine in neutral and drift in. If the boat has too much headway, on the other hand, reverse the engine briefly to stop it in the water and then drift down on the dock. Begin your drift when the distance between boat and dock is between one and two boat widths. Cut the engine after a bow line has been made fast, and then put out a stern line to the dock.

Many outboard skippers consider fenders an unnecessary nuisance. Be wise, and recognize that repairing a scraped and banged-up hull is much more of a nuisance. Fenders are inexpensive and handy insurance against costly repairs. Use them.

Very often you will find the wind and/or current moving toward a dock, but at an angle. When confronted with this situation, attempt to head the boat into the wind or current before coming to a stop and drifting down on the dock. This way, if anything goes wrong, the boat is headed out and can be pulled clear easily.

Docking is less difficult when the wind and/or current are moving off the dock. Here, if a poor approach is made, the boat will be carried clear rather than slammed into the dock. With fenders in place, approach the dock as shown in Figure 56(A), coming in at a fairly sharp angle. Throttle down to the lowest speed that still permits you to steer and make contact with the bow. Have a crew member or someone on the

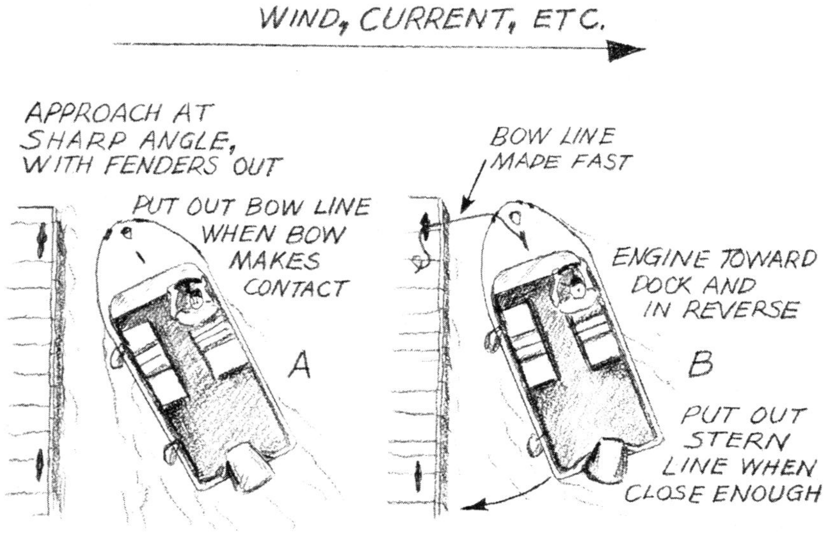

WIND, CURRENT, ETC.

APPROACH AT
SHARP ANGLE,
WITH FENDERS OUT

PUT OUT BOW LINE
WHEN BOW
MAKES
CONTACT

A

BOW LINE
MADE FAST

ENGINE TOWARD
DOCK AND
IN REVERSE

B

PUT OUT
STERN
LINE WHEN
CLOSE ENOUGH

Figure 56. How to approach a dock with the wind and/or current moving away from the dock.

dock make the bow line fast. Put the engine in neutral. At this point, turn the engine toward the dock, put it in reverse, and pull the stern in to the dock [Figure 56(B)]. When the boat is parallel to the dock, put out a stern line and cut the engine.

If the wind is coming off a dock at an angle, always head into it when approaching. In this case also the trick is to gently ease the bow up to the dock, make a bow line fast, and then bring the stern in as described above.

With docking space becoming increasingly scarce, outboard boatmen are finding that they have less choice when it comes time to tie up. This means that you must be able to maneuver your boat into and out of slips as well as to and from moorings and docks. Getting into and out of a slip requires skillful boat handling, but it is easily mastered with a bit of practice.

When wind and current are no problem, entering a slip is easy. Simply line the boat up parallel with the slip before entering. Avoid entering at an angle, if you want to keep from banging up the hull. Then, with the engine throttled down and fenders in place, move into the slip. Bring the boat to a stop by reversing the engine briefly, and put out bow and stern lines.

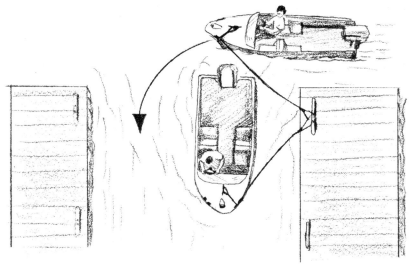

Figure 57. Using a bow line to ease the boat forward into a slip. If the wind is strong enough to blow the stern across the slip entrance, simply run a stern line to the same cleat as the bow line, and then pivot the boat into place.

If wind and/or current, however, are likely to give trouble when entering a slip, a bow line can be used to pivot the boat into the slip. See Figure 57. First approach the slip at right angles to it and put out the bow line to the cleat or piling at the slip's mouth. The length of line put out should be about two feet less than the width of the slip. Continue forward at idling speed until the line is taut, and then head the boat into the slip. The bow line will pivot the boat into position parallel to the slip. At this point cast off the bow line, straighten the engine, ease forward into position, and then tie up.

If the wind and/or current are strong enough to push the stern across the slip's mouth and into the opposite dock during the pivoting maneuver, another line is needed. Simply put out a stern line to the same cleat the bow line is fastened to. Then, when the boat is pivoted into the slip, the stern will be held in place. Easing the bow line after the boat is parallel to the slip allows it to move forward into place.

Wind and/or current must also be taken into account when leaving a slip. Play it smart and analyze their effect before casting off, and you will avoid both potential damage to the boat and the possibility of acute embarrassment. If there is no wind or current problem, simply back straight out of the slip until the boat is completely clear. Then, operating

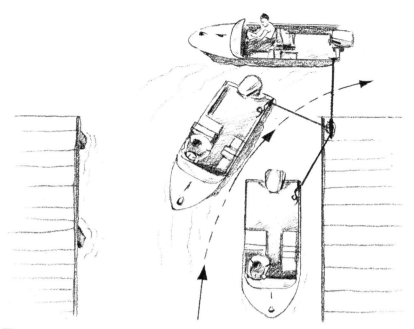

Figure 58. Using a stern line to pivot the boat clear of a slip. Be sure the line is fastened to the cleat on the dock so that it can be pulled free when desired.

at low speed, turn the boat and steer away from the area of the slips.

If there isn't room to back out safely, or if wind and/or current pose a problem, use a stern line to pivot the boat clear of the slip. See Figure 58. Fasten the stern line, which should be about two thirds the length of the boat, to a cleat at the corner of the slip. Next, back the boat out of the slip until the line goes taut. At this point, turn the engine to pivot the boat clear. When the boat is completely out of the slip, the stern line is freed. Steer the boat at idling speed clear of all obstacles before putting it on course and increasing speed.

TYING UP CORRECTLY

For a quick and easy lesson in how *not* to tie up to a dock or in a slip, just visit any busy marina. Many of the boatmen who pull in for supplies, ice, fuel, or what have you, will demonstrate an impressive variety of incorrect ways to tie up. A bow line and possibly a stern line will

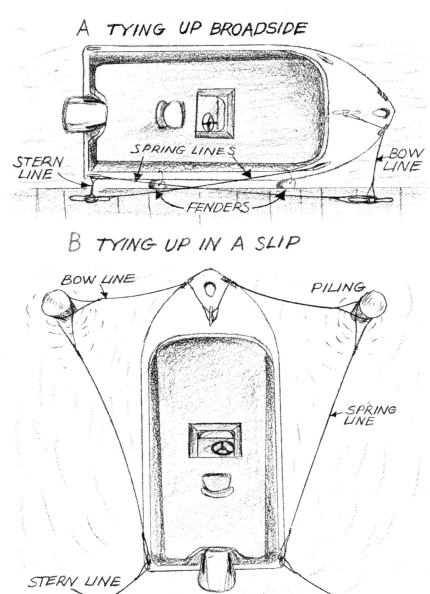

Figure 59. How to tie up broadside to a dock and in a slip. The lines must be placed carefully to prevent damage to the boat.

usually do for a short stay at the dock. (Now is a good time to review knots, hitches, and bends. Can you tie all of them?)

For a longer stay, the safety of the boat under a variety of conditions must be considered. For example, a wind shift may cause the boat to bang against the dock. The wakes of passing boats can also pose a problem; often a wake can set a docked boat swinging back and forth. If it is not tied up properly, damage to the hull may be the result.

Figure 59(A) shows the proper lines to use when mooring broadside. The *bow* and *stern* lines are made fast to the nearest cleat forward and aft. They hold the boat in position broadside to the dock. Bow and stern lines should never be set up tight in tidal waters. Enough slack must be allowed for the rise and fall of the tide.

The *spring lines* serve another purpose: They prevent the boat from surging back and forth at the dock. To be most effective, they should be as nearly parallel to the dock as possible. As Figure 59(A) shows, the *after spring line* runs from the foredeck cleat all the way to the dock cleat *aft* of the boat. The *forward spring line* then runs from a stern cleat to the dock cleat forward of the boat. Shorter spring lines may be used, but they become less effective as the angle between the line and the dock increases. You will often be tempted to skip the spring lines and make do with just the bow and stern lines. For a short stay in relatively quiet waters, this may be adequate. On the other hand, if there is any traffic in the channel near your boat and you intend to stay awhile, it is much wiser to rig the spring lines. For an overnight stay, the spring lines are a must. And don't forget fenders. Without them, you run the risk of badly scarring the finish on the hull.

Tying up in a slip, that is, stern to a dock with the bow between two pilings, poses an altogether different problem. In this case, the trick is to arrange the docking lines so that the boat is held off the dock, and also securely between the pilings. In addition, the stern must be held in place, so that it does not sway back and forth or into the adjacent slip.

Figure 59(B) shows how to rig the lines. First, note the arrangement of the stern lines. These are led from the stern cleats on the boat out parallel to the dock; if set properly, these lines prevent the stern from swaying from side to side. The spring lines are rigged from the stern cleats to the pilings. They hold the stern of the boat away from the dock. Finally, the bow lines should be at about right angles to the centerline of the boat to effectively hold the boat in position. It is sometimes quite difficult to tie up in a slip. Often the pilings are so far apart that reaching them becomes a problem. In addition, water turbulence may bob the boat about so that keeping your balance while tying up is difficult.

BEACHING

One of the great advantages of shallow-draft outboard boats is that they can be beached with ease. Thus, the skipper and crew enjoy the luxury of choosing just the right picnic or camping spot—be it a secluded stretch of white sandy beach or an abandoned island ripe for exploring.

Beaching an outboard is an easy maneuver. After you have chosen a good spot, throttle down the engine and head the boat in toward shore. The impulse will be strong to simply drive the boat ashore, cutting the engine and tipping it up at the last minute. Resist this impulse, unless you don't mind damage to the bottom of your boat. Instead, bring the boat to a stop in shallow water, step over the side, and walk it in after cutting the engine and tipping it up. If there is sufficient wave action to threaten the engine or stern of the boat, bring it in transom first.

A few simple precautions should be taken when beaching a boat. First, allow for tide. A boat beached at high tide is a real problem if, later on, it is high and dry. Choose an approach to the beach that is free of sharp rocks, if this is possible. Banging on rocks can seriously damage the bottom of a hull. Finally, if you beach at low tide, carry the anchor ashore and dig it into the ground well forward of the boat. It's surprising how many apparently capable outboard skippers have their boats drift away on the incoming tide.

SECURING THE BOAT

Your trip is over. The boat is moored, or tied up at dock. Skipper and crew are refreshed, but pleasantly fatigued, and ready to call it a day. The natural instinct at this point is to pick up personal gear and go home. The final tidying up that the boat obviously needs can be taken care of before the next outing. Don't yield to this temptation. If you let these "housekeeping" chores go, you face a dirty, cluttered, and generally un-shipshape boat when you are ready to go out the next time. The mess never seems like much when you leave it. When you come back, however, it seems much worse because it stands in the way of the pleasure you want right away—*not* after forty-five minutes or more of cleaning up. Pump and sponge out the bilge. Make fast all loose gear, such as paddles, life jackets, bilge pump, and cushions. Run the outboard engine dry, and tip it up out of the water.

Collect all trash and the leftovers from your picnic lunch. Do not throw any of this in the water. Virtually all marinas and yacht clubs supply large trash bins. Use them. There is nothing worse than a mooring area or marina fouled by floating garbage and trash. Clean up topsides and deck. Don't forget to take the "cooler" with you, especially if it contained fruit juice or iced tea. If it held fresh water, and there is some left over, salt-water boatmen should use it to sponge down the topside varnished woodwork. This removes the salt residue and prolongs the life of the varnish.

Finally, make a last check to be sure the mooring line is securely fastened and that it runs through a bow chock. Also make sure the mooring float is tightly lashed down on the foredeck. The last task before leaving the boat is fastening the cockpit cover in place. If you are tied up at a dock or in a slip, check the docking lines one last time.

That does it. The boat is now in shipshape condition. You can go home confident that you have done everything possible to prevent damage between outings. You also know that everything is ready to go the next time you go out.

OUTBOARDING ON RIVERS

The outboard skipper who takes his boat to a river will find conditions quite different from those found on the open seas and lakes. Strong winds and heavy seas, for example, are seldom encountered. Instead, strong currents, an ever-changing bottom, and the possibility of underwater obstructions lurk in every apparently smooth and quiet river. What is worse, these problems vary in intensity from river to river. No two rivers are alike; as a result, maintaining safety standards is a constant challenge.

The first step in planning any river cruise, unless you use your boat in the area every day, is to get all the information available about the river. Obtain the appropriate charts, and then check with the local authorities for any changes you should know of. Find out, if you can, any recent

Figure 60. The boat is beached, and the boys are enjoying a pleasant and private swim. But did they suck sand or silt into the cooling system before cutting the engine? And shouldn't the engine be tipped up to protect the propeller? And finally, shouldn't the anchor be set out to keep the boat from drifting away? (*Photo courtesy of Kiekhaefer Mercury.*)

changes in the river's bottom. Strong currents carry silt, debris, and dirt downstream, alternately picking this material up and depositing it as the river bends and changes depth.

For the most part, plan to do your boating near the center of the river, or in the marked channels. Do not cut corners, for sandbars and silt flats build up at bends and at the junction of rivers. Take care, however, when directly upstream and downstream of an island in the center of a river. Shoals build up above and below islands, and often extend long distances. Although there is no sure way to tell shallow water from deep water, you will find that shallow water is often lighter in color, ripples more in the wind, and may become quite choppy when it is extremely shallow.

An anchor and sufficient line are a must for river boating. If you run out of gas or your engine quits, the anchor is the only way to stop the boat short of running aground or colliding with some fixed obstacle in the water. Take care too when anchoring overnight. If you anchor in shallow water, you may be aground in the morning because of water flow regulation at a nearby dam or lock. Anchoring within or near the channel, on the other hand, exposes the boat to floating debris and the possibility of being rammed by another boat.

There are a few hazards unique to river boating. For example, pass well clear of fixed objects when traveling in heavy currents. If you pass too close, your boat may be pulled into or under the object. This is caused by a phenomenon called the Venturi effect; it occurs when a rapid current passes between two objects. In essence, a pressure difference forces the objects to move toward each other.

Large barge tows constitute a hazard also to the unwary boatman. To begin with, if you get too close to the side of a large tow, the suction currents of the Venturi effect may pull the boat into the tow, or perhaps into the propellers of the tug. Stay away from the front of a tow also, for there is a blind area in the pilot's line of view. A stalled boat, a man overboard, or a dumped water skier may not be seen in time to prevent an accident. Because of the current, stay clear also from the area upstream of a moored barge. It takes just a moment for a boat to be trapped and pulled under the barge by the current.

Many large bodies of water used for boating are impounded by dams. Both sides of a dam are dangerous for small boats. Strong currents above a dam can draw boats into the water intakes. Below a dam, the turbulence at the discharge outlets can be extremely hazardous.

LOCKS

Sooner or later the boatman operating on river waters will have to pass through a lock. This is not a particularly difficult task, however, if a few simple rules are followed. To begin with, plan ahead and learn the local rules. In addition, do exactly as you are instructed by the operator of the lock. When entering a lock, be sure fenders are set out to protect the side of the boat, wear a life jacket while handling lines, and rig all lines so they can be broken free when necessary. Cast off only when you get the signal, and then leave the lock at reduced speed. Note that when commercial river traffic is heavy, pleasure boats have a low priority at locks. Avoid delay by finding out beforehand just what the locking conditions ahead are.

8.   ANCHORS AND ANCHORING

ANCHORING IS AN IMPORTANT PART of boating. All boats should have at least one anchor aboard, together with enough line for the waters on which the boat customarily operates. Although one anchor is usually enough for smaller boats, at least two should be kept aboard larger boats. In the absence of a better rule, for temporary daytime anchoring plan to use about one-half pound of anchor for each foot of boat length. For example, a nine- or ten-pound Danforth anchor would be quite adequate for an eighteen-to-twenty-foot boat during a picnic lunch under relatively good conditions. On the other hand, a larger boat anchoring overnight should use a heavier anchor to guard against dragging while the crew is asleep. Boatmen often refer to their lighter anchor as the "lunch hook." Not many are willing to sleep over on a lunch hook; there is too great a possibility of dragging.

As you probably have gathered by now, there is more to anchoring than just tossing a weight on a line overboard. Many factors must be taken into account when anchoring. What does the bottom consist of? Is it rocky, sandy, or covered with seaweed or mud? Is the anchor to be used correct for the type of bottom? How deep is the water? Is there enough anchor line to give adequate *scope* (the length of anchor line needed for the anchor to hold), particularly when the tide comes in? How will the boat swing around in relation to other anchored boats should the wind or tide change? Is the spot chosen for anchoring protected from the wind and sea? If you satisfy yourself on all these counts, the chances are that you will be safely and securely anchored.

TYPES OF GROUND TACKLE

Many types of anchors are available. We have chosen to describe four of the more popular types. These are anchors you are likely to see in use on small boats. They have different characteristics, all of which must be considered when an anchor is chosen.

The *yachtsman's* anchor, although awkward to handle and store, offers the best holding power in various types of bottom. It is particularly good in a rocky bottom. This anchor is somewhat heavier than other more modern anchors for the same holding power. The drawing shows the yachtsman's anchor opened for use and folded down for storage. The *Danforth* anchor has exceptionally good holding power, although it is quite light in weight. For this reason, it has become very popular. As you shop around for an anchor, you will discover many that are simple variations of the Danforth idea. For a general-purpose anchor for sandy or muddy bottom, the Danforth is your best choice.

Two types of *mushroom* anchors are shown in Figure 61. The anchor on many permanent moorings is a very large and heavy mushroom. Two other types are often seen on small boats. One has a long, thin shank, the other a short, stubby shank. Mushrooms are easy to use because there are no flukes for the anchor line to tangle on. In addition, they hold well in muddy bottoms. Many skippers of small racing sailboats carry a mushroom anchor. This anchor is used in a race to prevent drifting when the wind drops and the tide is running the wrong way. The *navy*-type anchor is shown here because it is often offered for sale to small-boat owners. It should not, however, be used on small boats. This type of anchor depends more on weight than on digging in for holding power. As a result, it is more useful on larger vessels. In the smaller sizes, the short flukes do not dig deeply enough to hold well. Thus the anchor simply drags through the surface layers of mud or sand.

CHOOSING AN ANCHORAGE

Unless you know a location thoroughly, deciding where to "drop the hook" can be a problem. Despite the unknown factors of a strange anchorage, however, there are certain guidelines that will help you whenever you wish to anchor. First, very carefully survey the harbor or bay you have selected. This means cruising slowly around the anchorage

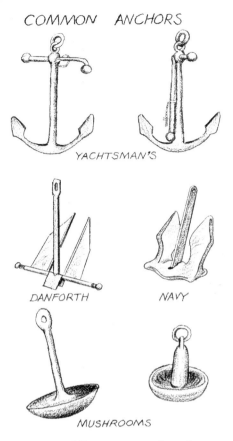

COMMON ANCHORS

YACHTSMAN'S

DANFORTH   NAVY

MUSHROOMS

Figure 61. A few of the different types of anchors now in use. For a
sandy or muddy bottom, the Danforth holds best and is the lightest.

until you know its characteristics, and until you find the quiet and
sheltered side. You should select a spot that is protected from the prevailing winds as well as from the larger waves that sweep into the harbor
from open water. Check the weather report for wind velocity and direction. This, of course, will have a bearing on where you anchor. For example, if the prevailing winds are southwest, you would ordinarily look
for a spot to the northeast of a group of small islands. But suppose an
easterly wind or storm is predicted. Under these circumstances an
anchorage northeast of an island would be exposed to the predicted
weather. Your stay would be uncomfortable at least, and possibly dangerous should the wind really kick up.

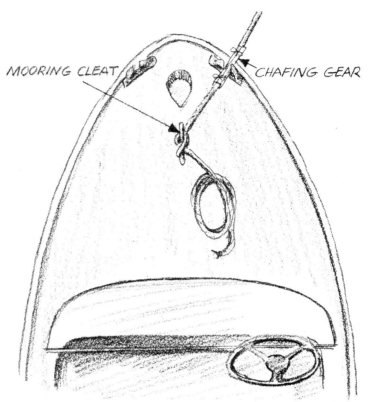

MOORING CLEAT   CHAFING GEAR

Figure 62. How to secure the anchor line. If the boat is to remain at anchor for any length of time, chafing gear should be used at the bow chock.

If you are in a small boat, look for a spot close to shore. Since boats with deep keels cannot anchor too close to shore, you should find plenty of room. If it becomes necessary, however, to anchor among other boats, choose a spot among boats the same size as your own. Try to anchor at least three to four boat lengths away from the nearest boat. This will allow enough room for swinging on the wind or tide.

Whenever possible, you should also study a chart of the anchorage area before selecting a spot. The chart will indicate the depth of the water at low tide and the nature of the bottom. As you well realize, both factors are important. It is rather senseless, for example, to expect a Danforth anchor to hold on a rocky bottom when the obvious choice is the yachtsman's anchor.

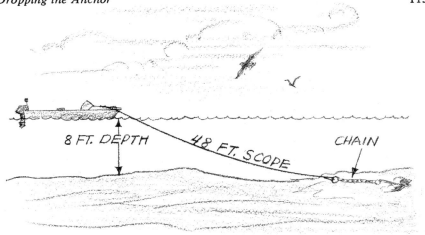

Figure 63. Scope is the length of anchor line compared to the depth of the water. For most types of bottom, a scope of six to one is adequate. The length of chain holds the shank of the anchor parallel to the bottom so that the flukes can take a firm hold.

DROPPING THE ANCHOR

For some obscure reason most boating beginners think the way to put an anchor down is to throw it as far away from the boat as possible. This is incorrect. Whenever an anchor is thrown, there is a possibility the line will foul on the flukes; as a result, the anchor will not take hold. A good seaman makes sure the anchor line is fastened to the boat (Figure 62), frees the line on deck to avoid entanglement, and then *lowers* the anchor over the side when the skipper gives the command.

The sequence of steps is quite simple, and is easy to master. The skipper puts his crew forward to handle anchor and line just as soon as he has chosen a spot. He then heads the boat up into the wind (or the current, whichever prevails; check other anchored outboard craft in the area) so that it stops dead in the water directly over the spot selected. At his command, the crew then lowers the anchor to the bottom and pays out the line as the boat is gently powered backward. After he has paid out enough line to equal three or four times the depth of the water, he holds (*snubs*) the line momentarily to make the anchor dig in. Enough additional line is then paid out to get the correct *scope,* and the line is cleated down.

SCOPE

If you will look back at the drawings of anchors, you will see that it is necessary for the shank of most anchors to be parallel to the bottom for the flukes to take hold. But the shank can only remain parallel to the bottom if the pull of the anchor line is sideways. A sideways pull can be accomplished one way only. This is by paying out enough anchor line so that it lies parallel to the bottom where it ties into the anchor. It generally takes a length of line from four to seven times the depth of the water to insure that the anchor will hold. This length of line is called the *scope*. If there is any doubt about whether an anchor will hold, the wisest move is to increase scope. Of course, if other anchored boats are too close, there is a limit to the amount of scope you can use.

As you can see, the trick is to prevent any upward pull on the shank of the anchor. Increasing scope will do it. But there is another way also. This is to add weight to the anchor line so that it holds the anchor's shank down. Figure 63 shows a popular way to do the job. Simply add a short length of galvanized chain between the anchor and anchor line. About four to six feet of quarter-inch chain should work quite well for an eighteen-to-twenty-foot boat. Marine supply stores, in fact, sell such lengths of chain coated with rubber. The rubber protects the iron from rusting and also keeps the chain from scarring the finish of the boat.

Keep in mind that you drop the anchor some four to six times the depth of the water forward of the spot you have chosen for the boat. That is, the boat will ride below the point where the anchor is actually dropped overboard. If your judgment is good, the boat will come to rest close to the three to four boat lengths from the nearest boat that you planned on. If your judgment is poor, you will have to try again. Every anchorage has its inept skipper—the fellow who never succeeds in anchoring his boat free of other boats.

Let's assume you have the anchor down and that you think there is enough scope for it to hold. How do you make sure? The answer is simple: Take *bearings* on shore to see if the boat moves. Figure 64 shows how this is done. Look directly abeam of the boat and line up two objects on shore. Remember the two objects, and then check their position in fifteen minutes or so. If they remain in line, the anchor is not dragging. Check every hour or so, and if the boat swings on the tide or wind, take new bearings after it has come to its new position.

TAKING A BEARING ON SHORE
TO MAKE SURE ANCHOR ISN'T
DRAGGING

Figure 64. Taking a bearing to check position while at anchor. Line up two objects abeam of the boat and check periodically to make sure the bearing has not changed.

WEIGHING ANCHOR

Leaving an anchorage is similar to leaving a mooring, with one or two minor differences. The first thing to do is to start the engine. The crew should then go forward to haul in the anchor line until it is very nearly vertical. At this point the engine should be put in gear at idling speed. Next have the crew haul up the anchor, but do not take it on deck immediately. Dunk the anchor in the water to wash the mud away, or even swab it away. Take the anchor on deck only after it has been thoroughly cleaned, and then coil the anchor line and stow it with the anchor.

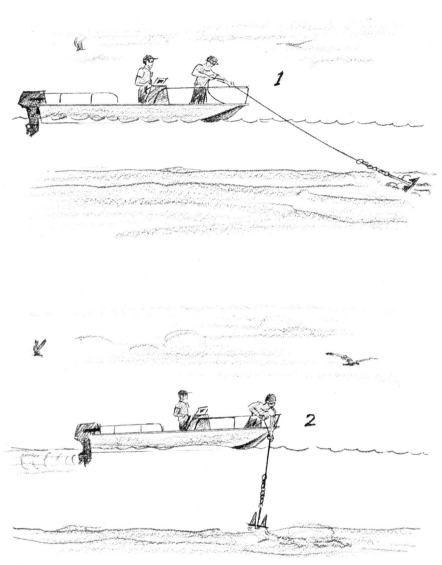

Figure 65. The steps in weighing anchor. Start the engine first and then heave in anchor line until the line is nearly vertical in the water. Next, haul up the anchor with the engine in gear at idling speed. Once the anchor is clear of the water the boat can be put on course.

Once the anchor is clear of the water, the skipper can gently accelerate the engine and steer to the desired course. Please note that all power boats should move very slowly in crowded anchorages, for the wake produced at higher speeds is very disturbing to people aboard craft at anchor.

Sometimes, if you have been anchored in a very muddy bottom, the anchor sticks tight. Despite hauling on the anchor line by skipper and crew, it won't come out. This is indeed a problem, but it is readily solved by using the engine. First, haul in the anchor line until it is vertical. Then cleat the line securely on deck and ease the boat ahead under power to break out the anchor. At this point stop the boat until the anchor is brought free of the water. Wait until the anchor is aboard before accelerating the engine and steering to the desired course.

9. READING THE WEATHER

THERE IS AN OLD SAYING that goes as follows: "The good seaman weathers the storm he cannot avoid, and he avoids the storm he cannot weather." We want to emphasize the importance of learning how to "read" the weather. If there is one single factor that dominates boating, it is the weather. Thus the knowledgeable boatman is always prepared on three counts: (1) he never goes out without obtaining the lastest weather report; (2) while on the water, he continually watches for indications of an adverse weather change; and (3) when such a weather change seems probable, he takes appropriate action at once. He does not wait, thinking (usually incorrectly) that the change won't occur for a while, or that he has plenty of time before the storm or squall hits.

Keeping on top of the weather is by no means as difficult as it may seem. This is particularly true of obtaining weather reports before going out, for a number of sources are readily available. Virtually every newspaper contains a daily weather map that gives the weather situation throughout the entire country. What is just as important, however, is that these maps allow rough-weather predictions for up to a day or so in advance. Become familiar with the map in your local paper. Learn the symbols, and study the map daily for a period of weeks or months. This will establish in your mind the normal weather patterns for your area, and enable you to make a reasonably good prediction on any given day. Television weather reports and forecasts are even better, for they provide a more up-to-date analysis of the local situation. Many of these programs, as you know, include a thorough weather-map analysis. If you plan to go

Figure 66. This photograph of hurricane Gladys (October 1968) taken from the *Apollo 7* spacecraft clearly shows the counterclockwise movement of the air mass around the "eye" of the storm. The photograph was taken about 150 miles southwest of Tampa, Florida, at an altitude of 97 nautical miles. (*Photo courtesy of NASA.*)

boating the following day, make it a practice to watch the TV weather report the night before. Radio forecasts are also important. You are no doubt familiar with the brief forecasts given often during regular programming. What you may not know is that many stations in coastal areas broadcast periodic marine weather forecasts. These reports are quite thorough, and they are essential to the careful boatman. If you cannot find station listings for marine forecasts in the paper, call your local Coast Guard station for the necessary information.

A good barometer is also very useful. This instrument, as you probably know, measures the pressure exerted by the atmosphere. In general, the drier the air, the greater the pressure it exerts. A rising barometer often means clearing, with fair weather ahead. A falling barometer, on the other hand, usually means bad weather, with rain and cloudy conditions. Do not rely on a barometer if you have access to other, more reliable sources of weather information. A barometer allows a very rough forecast only; it should not be looked upon as an infallible instrument. As you will see later in this chapter, clouds are good indicators also of what the weather holds. There are many different types of clouds, although just three types are enough to provide visible evidence of what is taking place, and what is likely to take place shortly. Cloud changes, in particular, are useful for signaling weather changes while you are out on the water. In fact, if you have been out for many hours, and you do not have a radio on board, changes in the cloud formations are probably the only indication of an impending weather change. We will shortly see just how.

WEATHER PATTERNS

Weather systems in the United States move from west to east. This general movement is caused by the westerlies—prevailing winds that result from the earth's rotation. In addition, the heating effect of the sun and the interaction of high- and low-pressure areas produce weather changes.

As you may know, the weather we experience is the result of alternating high- and low-pressure areas passing overhead. That is, "lows" are usually followed by "highs." When the pressure is high, the weather is generally good. On the other hand, the weather is usually poor when a low is centered overhead.

Highs and lows are characterized by a particular type of air movement. As Figure 67 shows, the wind blows in a clockwise direction around a high, but also toward the outside. This is called *anticyclonic rotation*. The wind around a low, on the other hand, blows in a counterclockwise direction in toward the low-pressure center. This movement is called *cyclonic rotation*. A hurricane is simply a cyclonic storm of great intensity. As the warm moist air rotates toward the center of any low system, the air begins to rise. But in rising it is cooled. Then, when sufficient cooling has occurred, moisture condenses and clouds and rain result.

A closer look at Figure 67 will suggest one or two additional clues to the weather. For example, along the East Coast strong northeast winds usually mean increasing cloudiness and rain. In New England such storm sys-

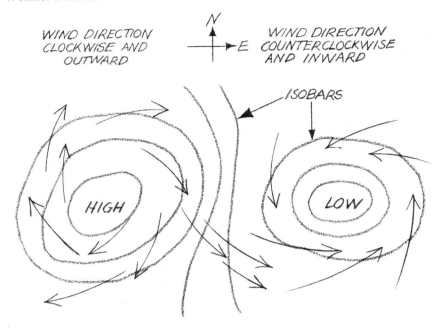

WIND DIRECTION
CLOCKWISE AND
OUTWARD

N

E

WIND DIRECTION
COUNTERCLOCKWISE
AND INWARD

ISOBARS

HIGH

LOW

Figure 67. Weather patterns flow from west to east across the country, with high-pressure areas alternating with low-pressure areas. Note how the winds blow around highs and lows. An isobar is a line drawn through points of equal barometric pressure.

tems are referred to as "nor'easters." When the wind then shifts to northwest, it usually means the passage of a low and the approach of a high. Clearing generally follows, and fair weather can be expected until the next low arrives. Note that wind direction is given as the direction from which the wind comes. For example, a northeast wind is blowing from the northeast.

So far we have described the air mass movements that produce weather changes over very wide areas. The wind of a nor'easter and the brisk northwest breeze that follows passage of a cold front are results of these major air movements. On a smaller scale, the boatman can look also for two types of local breezes, both of which can affect his boating pleasure. These two breezes are called the *land breeze* and the *sea breeze*.

Land and sea breezes occur near the coastline. Indeed, the story is that the fore-and-aft rigs of modern sailboats were originally developed in this country to take advantage of the land and sea breezes along our seacoasts and on the Great Lakes. These breezes develop because water and land differ in their capacity to absorb and hold heat, and because the air above is warmed up or cooled in terms of the water or land temperature beneath. Water absorbs heat from the sun much more slowly than land, but it also holds the heat much longer.

Let's start our description at a point in time when the water and land temperatures are about the same—an hour or so before midnight. As the night hours pass, the land continues to cool. The water just offshore, however, does not lose heat as fast. The result is that around midnight the air above the water is warmer than the air above the adjacent land area. But warm air rises. Thus the air above the water rises, and the cooler air over the land area moves in beneath it. This cool air in motion off the land is the land breeze. See Figure 68. Of course, as the cool air comes in contact with the warmer water, it is also warmed. It then rises, and the cycle continues.

After sunrise, the land warms up rapidly. On a bright, sunny day it is usually warmer than the adjacent water sometime around noon. At this point the warm air over the land rises, cooler air moves off the water to take its place, and a sea breeze begins. See Figure 69. Anyone who has been to the beach on a bright, warm day is familiar with sea breezes. They usually blow briskly through the afternoon, and then die down around sundown. The greater the temperature difference between land and water, the stronger the breeze.

Many sailors have learned to depend upon afternoon sea breezes to get them home. On Long Island Sound, for example, the afternoon sea breeze from the south is practically a tradition. Local sailors call it the "homing" breeze; they are greatly disappointed if it does not appear "on time" to get them into port before dusk.

FRONTS

With major air masses rotating around highs and lows, contact between two masses of air with differing temperatures is inevitable. Such a collision is called a *front*. There are four types of front: *cold, warm, occluded,* and *stationary*.

As far as the boatman is concerned, the cold front is the most important, for it is usually accompanied by violent thunderstorms. A cold front is produced when a cold air mass meets and thrusts under a warm air

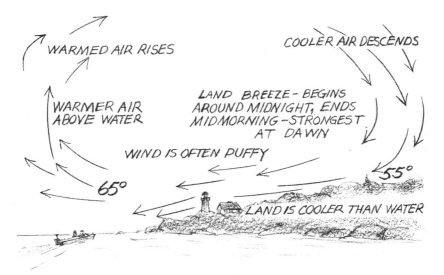

Figure 68. How a land breeze is generated. The warmer air above the water rises, and the cooler air above the land moves under it.

Figure 69. How a sea breeze is generated. The warmer air above the land rises, then the cooler air over the water moves in under it. Late-afternoon sea breezes are often a great help to sailors heading back to home port.

mass. Because the colder air is heavier, it stays close to the ground, but forces the warm, moist air rapidly to high altitudes. As the warm air rises and cools, its moisture condenses, forming thunderhead clouds. Severe thunderstorms often result. The formation of thunderhead clouds along a cold front is shown in Figure 70.

A warm front results when warm air rides up and over a mass of cold air. The warm air, usually laden with moisture, then cools, and the moisture condenses. Cloudiness and rain are the result. Sometimes a fast-moving cold front will overtake a warm front moving in the same direction. When this happens, the cold air in front of and behind the warm air forces the warm air upward. This is called an occluded front. Such fronts may behave as cold fronts or warm fronts or both. Finally, when a cold front and a warm front meet head on and interlock, the result is a stationary front. It helps to know the type of weather that frontal conditions will bring. In particular, you should be wary of any approaching cold front, for the thunderstorms it brings are often very severe and dangerous.

CLOUDS AND STORMS

Of the many different cloud types, three are of particular importance to the boatman. These are the *cumulonimbus,* or thunderhead; the *cumulus;* and the *cirrus* clouds. Cumulonimbus clouds are the massive vertical thunderhead clouds associated with the violent thunderstorms mentioned earlier. All boatmen must learn to recognize these clouds, for the storms they bring can be very dangerous to boats.

Typical thunderstorms occur during the summer months, usually late in the day. These storms make their first appearance as a darkening sky, usually in the northwest. Often, however, the first warning of an approaching thunderstorm may be AM radio static. Static may develop up to ten hours prior to the storm itself. Following the darkening sky, the typical anvil-shaped, towering thunderhead appears. The cloud is dark and "dirty" along its bottom, with violent wind gusts, heavy rain, and whitecaps underneath. The top is anvil-shaped, but sometimes the cloud is so tall this formation isn't visible. Very often such a storm advances in a sharply defined front—an awesome sight to anyone who has witnessed it at sea.

When the storm hits, usually no more than a half hour after one sights the thunderhead, there will be violent winds from several directions and

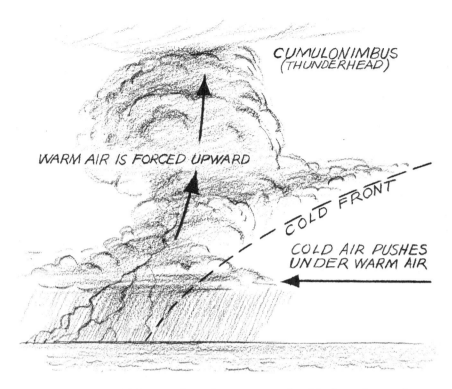

CUMULONIMBUS
(THUNDERHEAD)

WARM AIR IS FORCED UPWARD

COLD FRONT

COLD AIR PUSHES
UNDER WARM AIR

Figure 70. A cold front exists when a mass of cold air pushes under a mass of warmer air. As the warmer air rises, violent thunderstorms often develop.

usually a drenching rain. In one thunderstorm we rode out at anchor, the rain was so heavy it was impossible to see the stern of the boat from the cabin—a distance of some seven feet! Waves are generally not a problem, for these storms come up too quickly to generate much wave action. There are exceptions, however.

The winds in a thunderstorm are so violent and erratic it is very important to prepare properly for the arrival of the storm. *Under no circumstances should you attempt to continue on course through a thunderstorm.* If you are close enough to shore—be it a sandy beach, a sheltered cove, or home port—get in as quickly as possible. If there isn't time to reach shore or home port, slow down until you are just making headway and point the boat into the wind and waves. This may take you a bit off course, but it is far safer than running the risk of taking a wave broadside. In addition, don't attempt to run before the wind. Any water taken over the stern can swamp the boat, kill the engine, or both. If the water is not too deep, it is often wise to anchor and stay put until the thunderstorm passes.

If the thunderstorms you are caught in are the result of isolated masses of hot air rising into colder air, you can expect them to pass over quickly. These are the typical late-afternoon storms of a hot summer day. Storms associated with a cold front, however, may take longer to clear out. As you may know, these storms are spread out along the entire cold front. They are more violent than the local thunderstorm, but they can be avoided, for an advancing cold front is usually forecast well ahead of its arrival.

Cumulus clouds are fair weather clouds. These are the bright, "cottony" clouds seen on fair, sunny days. They have softly rounded edges, but near the horizon they are flat along the bottom. As long as cumulus clouds are in the sky, there is little chance of any change in the weather. It pays to keep an eye on cumulus clouds, however. Sometimes one can grow tall enough to reach elevations where the temperature is below freezing. When this happens, the innocent fair weather cumulus cloud can develop into the dangerous cumulonimbus thunderhead cloud.

Cirrus clouds generally indicate a change in weather, usually for the worse. These clouds are thin and wispy. A sky with cirrus clouds is often called a "mare's tail" sky, because of its similarity to the feathery wisps of a streaming horse's tail. Cirrus clouds occur at altitudes of twenty thousand to twenty-five thousand feet. They often indicate cloudy, rainy weather within a day or so.

STORM WARNINGS

Always check the weather report before going out. In addition, check for storm warnings at a nearby yacht club or marina. Administered by the U. S. Weather Bureau, storm warning stations are located along the East and West Coasts, on the Great Lakes, and in Hawaii and Puerto Rico. The warnings consist of flags or pennants for the daytime and lights for nighttime. As Figure 72 shows, there are four warnings: *small craft, gale, storm,* and *hurricane.* You should commit these signals to memory, and never forget to check before leaving port.

The most important warning for the outboarder is the small-craft advisory. This signal, when posted, covers a wide range of wind and/or

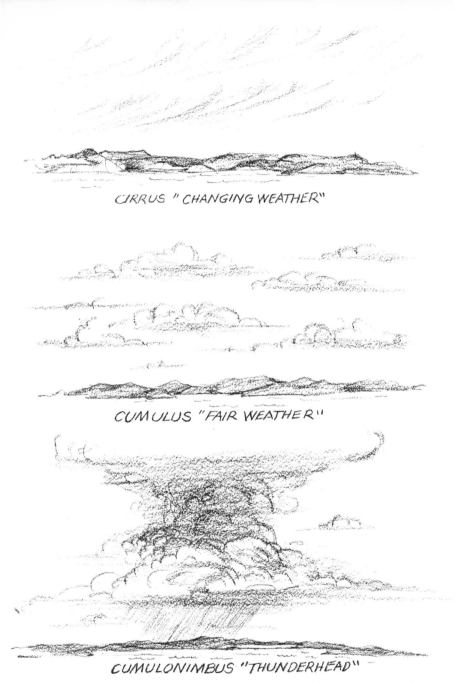

CIRRUS "CHANGING WEATHER"

CUMULUS "FAIR WEATHER"

CUMULONIMBUS "THUNDERHEAD"

Figure 71. The cloud shapes and patterns you should learn to recognize. It is especially important that you learn to spot thunderheads before the thunderstorm arrives.

sea conditions. In addition, the term "small craft" includes boats of many different sizes and types. To be on the safe side, always get a detailed weather forecast before going out when the small-craft advisory pennant is flying. Wind and sea conditions may or may not be too severe for your boat—you won't be able to tell from the warning signal alone. You will have to match experience with a detailed weather report to estimate the danger correctly. For example, on a given day, wind and sea conditions might be very hazardous for an open-cockpit twenty-foot runabout, but merely exciting and stimulating for a twenty-foot cruising boat with a deeper draft.

TIDE AND CURRENT

A brief word about the tides and the water movements they cause is in order at this point. Strictly speaking, *tide* is the vertical rise and fall of a body of water. Tide is caused by the gravitational pull of the moon, and to a lesser extent that of the sun, on a body of water. When the sun and the moon are in line with the earth, their combined pull is greater. Hence, the tidal range is greater. Such tides are called *spring tides*. On the other hand, when the sun, moon, and earth form a right angle in space—that is, when they are not in a line—the tidal range is smallest. These tides are called *neap tides*.

Knowledge of the behavior of the tides is an important factor in safe boating. Virtually every time he is on the water in his boat, the skipper will encounter some situation calling for knowledge of the time of high or low water, and of their approximate heights. He may be planning to anchor: Both the stage of the tide and its range will affect the scope chosen for the anchor line. He may want to cross a shoal area: The depth of the water will depend on the stage of the tide. He may want to tie up at a wharf or pier: The range of the tide will determine how he adjusts his lines.

The *Tide Tables,* published by the National Ocean Survey (formerly the U. S. Coast and Geodetic Survey), is the basic source of information on the tides. This volume, published anew each year, gives the time of high and low water, and the heights of the tides, for a number of important places called *reference stations*. Additional tables then give the differences in times and heights between the reference stations and thousands of other points called *subordinate stations*. "Local knowledge" is an important

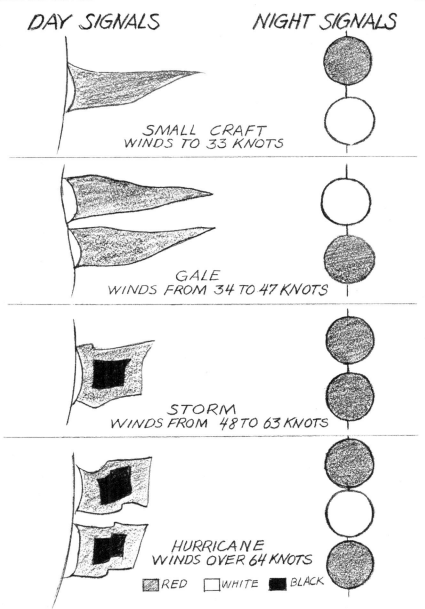

DAY SIGNALS   NIGHT SIGNALS

SMALL CRAFT
WINDS TO 33 KNOTS

GALE
WINDS FROM 34 TO 47 KNOTS

STORM
WINDS FROM 48 TO 63 KNOTS

HURRICANE
WINDS OVER 64 KNOTS

RED □ WHITE ■ BLACK

Figure 72. The official Weather Bureau Coastal Warning Display System. The night signals are lights. Be sure to get a complete weather forecast whenever small-craft advisories are displayed. It may be too rough for your boat.

supplement to the *Tide Tables*. If you are in unfamiliar waters, do not hesitate to ask experienced local boatmen for information. Firsthand local experience is often a far better predictor of what to expect than a set of tables.

As useful as the *Tide Tables* are, they give at best only an approximation of the actual tidal conditions. This is the case because certain unpredictable factors have a pronounced effect on the height of the tides. Atmospheric pressure is one of these factors. Water depths are given for a barometer reading of 29.92 inches of mercury. If the barometer reading falls below 29.92 inches, both high and low waters will be higher than predicted. The reverse is also true. If the barometer reading rises above 29.92 inches, the height of high and low waters will be lower than predicted by the tables. This effect is considerably greater than most people suspect. In fact, it is of the order of one foot of water depth for each inch of barometric pressure.

Another factor is wind. A steady wind blowing from seaward will literally pile up water in bays, inlets, and river mouths, making actual tidal levels higher than those predicted. A wind blowing toward the sea will of course have the opposite effect. In addition to the wind effect, the level of the water in tidal rivers is affected by changes in the volume of the flowing water. An abnormally fast snow melt-off in the watershed, or perhaps heavy rains upstream, can produce higher levels than those predicted. A dry spell, on the other hand, will have the opposite effect.

Caution is the watchword whenever you are using the *Tide Tables* for navigational purposes. It is especially important to be careful in operating a boat at low water. One or another, or perhaps combinations of the factors mentioned here, may act to reduce the water depth significantly below the predicted depth. For the unwary outboarder, this could lead to a load of silt or sand in the engine's cooling system, or perhaps a damaged propeller blade.

Current is the horizontal flow of water. When the tide changes at high tide, and the water begins to drop, it can only drop by flowing horizontally out of or away from the bay or inlet it had flooded. Current caused by tidal changes is called *tidal current*. The current of a river or stream is not associated in any way with the tide; it is caused by the earth's gravitational force only.

The effects of tidal currents should be taken into consideration by all boatmen who use coastal waters. Among the situations that may present a problem are a strong adverse current, the turbulence produced when two currents intermingle or converge, a current setting at an angle to a channel, and the often dangerous conditions produced when wind, current, and surf combine in inlets. The wise skipper entering unfamiliar waters will first consult the *Tidal Current Tables* (published by the National Ocean Survey), and then become as knowledgeable as he can about local conditions. He will look for evidence of currents at all stages of the tide, and make a point of remembering what he has seen. The ripples and wakes produced at dock piles and channel stakes, the angle of lean of buoys, and the directional patterns of anchored boats are all useful clues to current behavior.

It is very important that the small-boat skipper understand and compensate for the effect of current on a boat's progress. For a boat traveling in the same direction as the current, for example, the boat's speed over the bottom is increased by the speed of the current. The opposite effect is produced when a boat heads into an adverse current. Suppose an outboard is traveling at a speed of fifteen miles per hour through the water against an adverse current of four miles per hour. Under these conditions, the boat will be making a speed of only eleven miles per hour (fifteen miles per hour minus four miles per hour) over the bottom. It will therefore take longer for the boat to reach its destination. In addition, if the skipper has not anticipated the longer running time, there is the possibility that he will run out of fuel before arriving at his destination.

Tidal currents moving at an angle to the course of a boat pose a different problem. For example, a boat steering due north through a current flowing eastward will actually follow a northeasterly course over the bottom. In other words, as the boat travels north through the water, the current carries it in an easterly direction at the same time.

Most outboard-powered craft are capable of sufficient speed to overcome the effect of an adverse current. Nevertheless, the capable skipper learns the current patterns of the waters he does his boating on, and adjusts his departure times and courses steered to take advantage of, or at the very least, to minimize, the adverse effects of tidal currents.

10.   BOATING IN HEAVY WEATHER

SOONER OR LATER every outboard boatman, despite the routine precaution of checking the weather before leaving home port, finds himself out in rough weather. Obviously, there are certain dangers associated with boating under rough conditions. How such experiences turn out depends entirely upon three factors: (1) how well the boatman understands the various wind and sea conditions he can expect to meet; (2) how well he prepares himself, his crew, and his craft for heavy going; and (3) the physical limitations of his boat. All three are important. The sturdiest outboard is useless in a blow if the skipper fails to take measures to make it seaworthy.

WIND AND WAVE CONDITIONS

In general, waves are produced by wind. Over the ocean, strong storm winds build up the long waves commonly referred to as "swell." In addition to these, local winds produce the choppy conditions you are most likely to encounter in an outboard. The important point to remember is that strong winds produce potentially dangerous waves. Sometimes these conditions come up very suddenly. The alert skipper must be ready to cope with them when they occur.

Both strong winds and the waves they generate pose hazards to small boats. Let's look at the types of wind and wave conditions you can expect to meet, and then describe how they can be handled. With respect to wind, you can look for strong, steady winds, or strong, puffy winds. Strong, steady winds occur in large storms, but they may occur also during the clear weather that follows the passage of a cold front. These winds can usually be predicted in advance; thus you should be able to avoid them.

Strong, puffy winds are more hazardous, as well as more difficult to predict. These winds occur in thunderstorms and in the sudden squalls that boatmen run into so often during the passage of weather fronts. It is the changeability of puffy winds that causes difficulty. They vary from extremely strong to light, and they change direction rapidly. Thus, if the skipper is not alert, he may be capsized by a sudden puff from a different direction, especially if the boat's load is poorly distributed.

On sheltered waters, such as harbors and small lakes, the long waves of the open ocean are not present. When high winds blow for prolonged periods over shoal-water areas, however, steep, choppy waves often develop. Such waves can be particularly troublesome in the shallow water areas of underwater sand bars and adjacent to inlets and river mouths. These waves come from many different directions, and are often extremely steep and close together. It is very difficult to judge where the next wave will come from; thus the skipper must always be on the lookout.

What do you do when a sudden squall appears and is unavoidable? First, have everyone on board put on life jackets. Children who are not strong swimmers, it should be noted, should wear life jackets at all times when out on the water. And all small children should have life jackets on if the going is the least bit rough. When the squall hits the boat, throttle down to avoid slamming into oncoming waves, and head up into the wind. Take oncoming waves at a slight angle. This will reduce slamming also.

How do you judge when wind and wave conditions are too rugged for boating? This depends on the size and sturdiness of your boat, plus your seamanship ability. A reliable indicator, however, is the presence of whitecaps. The beginner in a small boat should consider staying in port or coming in at once if the water is covered with whitecaps.

For more experienced boatmen, it is possible to stay out under more strenuous conditions. Sailors, in fact, find some of their most exciting sailing in good, stiff breezes that tend to discourage outboarders.

THE BEAUFORT WIND SCALE

At this time, while the effect of wind on the water is fresh in your mind, it seems a good idea to introduce the wind force scale. Clearly, it is important that you know how winds of different strengths affect the sea. No doubt you have heard such terms as "moderate breeze," "whole gale," and "hurricane." When the wind is blowing at eleven to sixteen knots, for ex-

TABLE II—BEAUFORT WIND SCALE

Code Figure	Beaufort's Scale	Effect on Sea	Velocity (Knots)
0	Calm	Sea smooth, mirrorlike.	Less than 1
1	Light air	Some ripples, no foamy tops.	1–3
2	Light breeze	Small wavelets, tops appear glassy but do not break.	4–6
3	Gentle breeze	Large wavelets. Occasional whitecaps.	7–10
4	Moderate breeze	Small waves increasing in length. Frequent whitecaps.	11–16
5	Fresh breeze	Moderate waves further increasing in length. Many whitecaps with spray.	17–21
6	Strong breeze	Large waves beginning to appear. Whitecaps everywhere, much spray.	22–27

TABLE II—BEAUFORT WIND SCALE (cont'd.)

7	Moderate gale	Large breaking waves. Foam begins to be blown in streaks in direction of wind.	28–33
8	Fresh gale	Moderately high waves. Tops break off and are blown in direction of wind.	34–40
9	Strong gale	High waves. Heavy foam streaks blown by wind. Sea beginning to roll, and spray may interfere with visibility.	41–47
10	Whole gale	Very high waves. Sea appears white all over. Heavy rolling of seas. Visibility seriously affected.	48–55
11	Storm	Extremely high waves. Medium-sized ships become lost to view for long periods of time.	56–63
12–17	Hurricane	Air filled with foam and spray. Waves higher than forty-five feet. Sea completely white with driving spray. Visibility extremely limited.	64–118

ample, whitecaps first appear. This is a "moderate breeze" on the Beaufort Wind Scale. For boats under twelve feet in length, boating is potentially hazardous in a moderate breeze. In a "fresh breeze" (seventeen to twenty-one knots), the length of the waves has increased, and whitecaps cover the water. Gusts, however, are often considerably stronger than twenty-one knots. Sailboats sixteen to twenty feet in length usually do well under these conditions when skippered by skillful sailors, but the going is rough and wet. Small boats should not be out in winds in excess of twenty-one knots, for the danger may be too great.

Up until now the terms mentioned above—moderate breeze, whole gale, and hurricane—probably meant little to you, aside from the fact that they conveyed a general idea of what the weather was like. As the skipper of an outboard-powered boat, however, you will need to know much more about them, for you will make many decisions based on wind force and sea conditions. For example, do you go out or stay in port? Should everybody on board be wearing a life jacket? Is the boat trimmed properly for heavy seas? And so on.

Sea conditions are the result of wind action. Good seamen know the relationship between the two, and make correct decisions on the basis of this knowledge. Read the Beaufort Wind Scale carefully. It may help you avoid a dunking (at the least) or a mishap of major proportions (at the most).

HEAVY WEATHER BOATING TACTICS

Contrary to widespread popular opinion, the size of a boat has little bearing on its seaworthiness. Of much greater importance are the boat's design features and construction. It seems obvious, but experience dictates that we emphasize the importance of design limitations. Small boats are designed with specific purposes and wind and sea conditions in mind. Just as it is dangerous to exceed the load limitations of a boat, it is hazardous to venture into weather conditions beyond those for which the boat was designed and built. The wise skipper, for example, does not take a flat-bottomed skiff designed for river use out into the open ocean.

There is more to it, however, than sticking to the weather conditions your boat was designed for. It is important also to know the boat's behavior characteristics under rough sea conditions. The basic principles of handling small boats under adverse conditions apply to all small craft.

Each boat, however, will react differently in terms of how it is handled, its design, and the way it is loaded and trimmed. Experience is the best teacher. Reading about what to do or taking courses will give you the facts you need. It will then be necessary to apply these facts when the wind blows and the sea is up. Hopefully, as you gain experience on the water, you will be exposed gradually to a variety of sea conditions rather than to a whole gale the first time you run into rough weather.

WHAT TO DO IN HEAVY WEATHER

- Put on warm and waterproof clothing.
- Put on life jackets.
- Close all hatches, ports, and windows.
- Pump out the bilges, and keep them empty.
- Secure all loose gear.
- Break out emergency gear.
- Adjust load to keep boat as level as possible.
- Stay near shore where water is smoother.
- Avoid unnecessary changes in course.
- Update position on your chart.
- Prepare to head for sheltered waters
  if necessary.

High seas driven before the wind constitute the major problem of the small boatman when the going is rough. These wind-driven waves move in the same general direction as the wind producing them, and they follow each other with monotonous and threatening regularity. The skipper thus has a choice of heading into the waves, traveling broadside to them, or running before the sea.

Running head-on into high seas is generally safe if the boat's speed is adjusted to the sea conditions, the oncoming waves are taken at a slight angle, and the boat's load is trimmed properly. When oncoming waves are very steep, it is necessary to reduce speed to prevent pounding and also to avoid "racing" the propeller in air. The trick is to cut forward motion until the boat is just making headway, and then to steer into the waves at an angle of about forty-five degrees. The reduced speed gives the bow a chance to rise with each oncoming wave, rather than driving into it. In addition, lower speeds permit the propeller to stay in the water, and thus prevent the wild engine and propeller racing that occurs when the propeller breaks free of the water. Attacking the waves at an angle softens the slamming and pounding of driving into head seas, and eases strain on the hull.

Proper trim is a must when a boat is being driven into head seas. If there is too much weight forward, for example, the bow will tend to plunge rather than rise. The ultimate result of an open-cockpit outboard driving into head seas and taking solid water over the bow should be obvious to everyone. Too much weight aft, on the other hand, will cause the bow to fall off, and make it difficult to maintain course. In the extreme this would put the boat broadside to the waves in the trough—a highly vulnerable position. Outboard skippers should not hesitate to move crew and/or portable gear in order to achieve proper trim. Again, however, experience is the only reliable teacher. Just be sure to learn in moderate sea conditions, not in a gale.

Occasionally it is not possible to run into head seas, and the boat must be set on a course broadside to the swells. This might occur, for example, in an emergency calling for the quickest possible return to port. If you find yourself in this situation, prepare for a wild ride. The boat will roll heavily as it falls from crest into trough, and then surges back up to the crest of the next wave. You should know that this course of action is a dangerous maneuver, and that the possibility of a capsizal is greatly increased.

If you have a bit more time, or if running broadside to the swells is too dangerous in spite of the emergency, try tacking across the troughs. This is nothing more nor less than following a zigzag course instead of paralleling the seas. See Figure 73. On one tack, head into the waves at an angle of about forty-five degrees. Then make a ninety-degree turn away from the direction of the weather and take the seas broad on the boat's quarter. If the turns are made quickly, the boat will be broadside to the waves for only a few moments while in the trough. Tacking across the troughs is much safer than running broadside to the seas. It may take you a bit longer, but your chances of getting there will be greatly improved.

Running before the seas can be hazardous also, especially in an outboard-powered craft. Most outboard engines are mounted so low there is always danger of taking a large following sea over the stern. This could swamp the boat, or perhaps douse the engine. In either case the boat is at the mercy of the wind and waves.

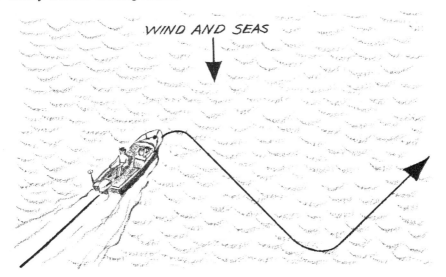

Figure 73. How to tack across the troughs to avoid running broadside to the seas.

Maintaining control of the boat is another problem. Often, when the helmsman is starting to run down the forward slope of a wave, the stern and propeller break free of the water, and he loses control of the boat. When this happens the boat may be thrown off course. This is called *yawing*. If the seas are particularly steep and violent, the boat may yaw to the point of *broaching*. In a broach, the boat is thrown broadside to the seas out of control. A capsizal often follows a broach, for the boat is essentially at the mercy of the seas until the helmsman regains steerage way.

Yawing can be reduced by slowing down to allow the seas to pass under the boat. This is easier on the engine, too, for there is less opportunity for the propeller to break free and race. An even better way to minimize the danger of running before the seas is to tack downwind, or before the seas. This maneuver is basically the same as tacking across the troughs, except that the zigzag course in this case always keeps the seas on the boat's quarter. This is shown in Figure 74. In summary, when it is necessary to go in the same direction as the wind and waves, slow down for better control of the boat, and tack downwind to avoid large waves directly astern.

If the action of the wind and waves becomes so strong that the boat threatens to go out of control, it is advisable to head into the wind and trail some sort of *sea anchor* from the bow. This will help to hold the bow of

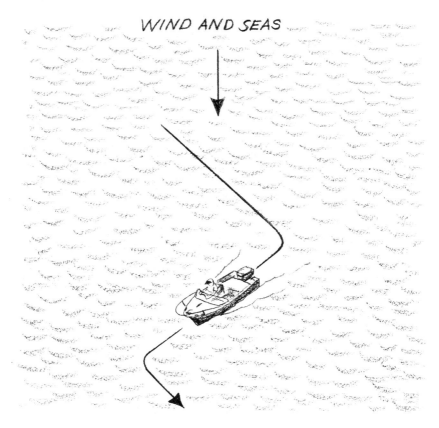

WIND AND SEAS

Figure 74. How to tack downwind to avoid running directly before the seas.

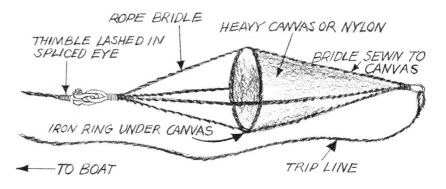

ROPE BRIDLE   HEAVY CANVAS OR NYLON

THIMBLE LASHED IN
SPLICED EYE

BRIDLE SEWN TO
CANVAS

IRON RING UNDER CANVAS

TO BOAT   TRIP LINE

Figure 75. A typical sea anchor. The trip line spills the anchor to vary the speed of drift of the boat and also to haul the anchor back aboard.

Figure 76. A sea anchor in use in very heavy seas. The anchor holds the boat's bow into the wind and waves, but permits a slow drift downwind.

the boat up into the wind, but at the same time permit a slow drift downwind. Prior to this step, which is in reality the last resort, the skipper should try *heaving to*. In this maneuver, the boat is headed into the wind and waves, and just enough power is used to maintain steerage way. The object is to keep the bow headed into the oncoming seas, but to reduce speed so that the strain on hull and passengers is reduced as much as possible.

Various types of sea anchors are available. One is shown in Figure 75. The drifting speed of a boat with a sea anchor out is controlled by the trip line of the anchor. By pulling on the trip line, you cause the anchor to spill, and the boat moves faster. See Figure 76. Anything dragged over the bow—a long line, a bucket, a swamped dinghy—serves as a sea anchor. Let's hope that you are never in the unfortunate position of requiring a sea anchor. In general, careful attention to the weather before going out can prevent such situations.

WHAT TO DO WHEN CAPSIZED

The commonest reaction to a capsizal, especially from beginners, is surprise. They all say they had no idea it was about to happen. Boats capsize for a variety of reasons. A sudden puff of wind, carelessness leading to a broach, and failure to balance crew weight are just a few. In the case of beginning boatmen, inexperience and misjudgment of wind and sea conditions are probably the most important factors.

We can't emphasize too strongly the importance of preventing a capsizal. In 1970, for example, of a total of 1,418 fatal boating accidents, 917 were caused by capsizing or falls overboard. The box summarizes

---

WHAT TO DO TO PREVENT A CAPSIZAL

- Reduce speed and head boat into oncoming seas.
- Secure all loose gear.
- Put out sea anchor, if required.
- Have all passengers put on life jackets.
- Stow all gear as low in boat as possible.
- Have passengers and crew sit on floor of cockpit.
- Anchor, if possible.

---

what you should do to minimize the chances of capsizing. Read its contents carefully. In a nautical paraphrase of Smokey the Bear, "Only *you* can prevent a capsizal." Unfortunately, capsizing can be as great a disaster as a forest fire in terms of loss of life. Very few people seem to know the correct things to do after they have been dumped into the water.

The most important rule is *Stay with the boat.* Obviously, this refers to a boat that will support the entire crew when it is swamped. A recent tragedy on Lake Michigan illustrates just how important this rule is. Two boys and a girl capsized in a small sailboat within view of about twenty people on shore. A rescue operation was started at once, but the only boat available had an engine that would not start. In the fifteen minutes it took to start the engine, both boys had drowned. They had started swimming for shore thinking that it was only a couple of hundred yards away. Both boys were excellent swimmers, but that "couple of hundred yards" turned out to be something over a mile. When the girl was finally picked up, she reported that one of the boys had called the other "chicken" because he had wanted to stay with the boat rather than strike out for shore.

Again and again lives are lost because people leave capsized boats. They panic and fail to realize that most boats will float even when swamped, and that it is far safer to stay with a swamped boat than to attempt to swim to shore. In many cases, it is possible to right the boat and then sit on the floor of the cockpit. In fact, the entire crew can often sit inside the cockpit of a swamped boat without sinking it.

In the unlikely event that a swamped boat isn't rescued right away, it may even be possible to bail it out. Hang on to the outside of the boat. If the waves are not too high, you may be able to splash and bail water from the cockpit fast enough to stay ahead of incoming water.

WHAT TO DO WHEN BOAT HAS CAPSIZED

- Swim back to boat at once.
- *Stay with the boat* if it remains afloat.
- Put on life jackets, take off footwear and excess clothing.
- Lash all loose gear together.
- Right boat if possible.

Bailing out a swamped boat is time-consuming and exhausting work, however, and should only be tried as a last resort. It is much better to save your strength and wait for rescue.

11. RULES OF THE ROAD AND AIDS TO NAVIGATION

ONE OF THE FIRST THINGS you will notice when you begin boating is the traffic. America's recreational waterways are becoming more and more crowded every year. Unfortunately, along with the crowding there has been a noticeable increase in the number of accidents. Thus, to enjoy boating and to avoid accidents, it becomes necessary to thoroughly master the traffic rules that govern the movements of boats. These regulations are called the rules of the road; their fundamental purpose is to avoid collisions. The rules apply to all types of boats, and cover all the possible types of meetings that can take place between two boats. In all these instances the rules determine the boat that is *privileged* and the boat that is *burdened*. A privileged boat has the *right of way,* is entitled to, and to a large extent is obligated to maintain course and speed. The burdened boat must look out for the privileged boat; it must alter course and/or speed so that it does not interfere with the progress of the privileged boat.

In almost all instances, a sailboat under sail alone has the right of way over a powerboat. This means that powerboats should stay clear of sailboats at all times. The important exceptions to this rule are as follows. A sailboat overtaking and passing a powerboat (or any boat, for that matter) is burdened; it must stay clear. Another exception refers to meetings in restricted channels. Neither sailboats nor powerboats under sixty-five feet in length can claim the right of way over large, powered vessels that can navigate only inside a restricted channel. The safest application of this rule for the outboarder is to attempt to stay clear of all other

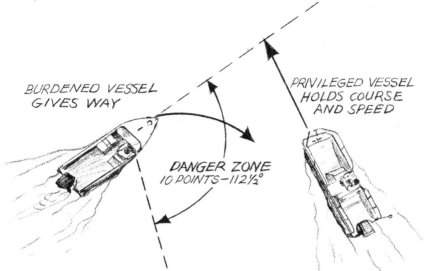

BURDENED VESSEL
GIVES WAY

PRIVILEGED VESSEL
HOLDS COURSE
AND SPEED

DANGER ZONE
10 POINTS—112½°

Figure 77. The "danger zone" rule of boats under power. Any boat that has another boat in its danger zone must give way. This means altering course, stopping, or even reversing, if necessary.

vessels when operating in a narrow channel. Finally, remember that all other vessels, including sailboats under sail alone, must stay clear of fishing vessels using nets or lines or trawls.

An informal rule that you should take to heart and employ whenever you are in doubt is as follows: *Don't press your advantage!* With the very large number of inexperienced boatmen now crowding the waterways, you cannot count on the other man knowing the rules or correctly anticipating your intentions. We repeat: If you are in doubt about the situation, make every attempt to stay clear. Such common sense and courtesy will go a long way toward making your hours on the water both happy and safe.

RULES FOR BOATS UNDER POWER

All boats using a form of mechanical propulsion are governed by these rules. This includes all powerboats, as well as sailboats using auxiliary power. Whenever a sailboat is powered by an engine—even if the sails are up—the boat is a powerboat according to the law and must follow the powerboat rules of the road. These rules differ from those for boats powered by sails alone. They are as follows: (1) *Two powerboats approaching each other head on should pass port side to port side.* When the skipper of one of the boats alters course to starboard to honor this rule, he should give one short blast on his horn. The other skipper should then acknowledge by returning the single short blast. In the event two boats are approaching each other and will pass starboard to starboard, two short blasts on the horn should be given to indicate that the course is being altered to port. Wherever possible, the boats should pass port side to port side, although instances do occur when it is more practical to pass starboard side to starboard side. In a special case, powerboats approaching each other on a river are subject to the following rule: The boat going downstream has the right of way over one going upstream. (2) *A boat having another boat in its danger zone (from dead ahead to two points abaft the starboard beam) must stay clear.* Figure 77 shows how the "danger zone" rule applies. It may even be necessary to stop or reverse direction to stay clear. (3) *Any boat leaving a slip, or a berth at a dock, has no rights until it is entirely clear.* This means that the boat leaving the slip or dock must consider itself burdened until it is completely clear of the dock and in open water. (4) *A powerboat overtaking another vessel must stay clear of the overtaken vessel.* When you are overtaking another vessel it is a matter of courtesy to pass in such a way that your wake does not adversely affect the overtaken boat. Some skippers apparently do not know, or perhaps they do not care, that they are responsible for any damage caused by their boat's wake.

It is important to note that when a boat is operating in reverse, its stern is considered the bow. This of course shifts the danger zone to the port side; it now runs from dead astern to two points forward of the port beam. One or two other points are worth noting. Powerboats should stay to the starboard side of narrow and winding channels whenever this is safe and practicable. If you are operating in fog, and hear a fog signal from someplace forward of your beam, stop engines, determine that you have running room ahead, and then proceed with extreme caution until all danger of collision has passed. The meeting and passing situations described here are illustrated in Figures 78 and 79.

Additional horn signals you should learn to recognize are (1) three short blasts—my boat is proceeding astern, and (2) four or more blasts—danger! (either an emergency or failure to understand another vessel's signal).

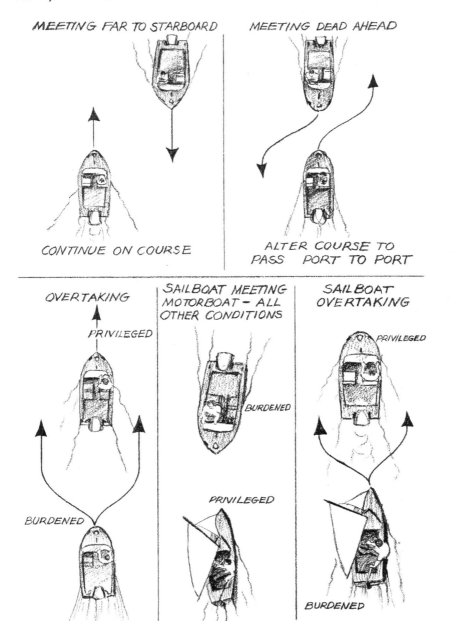

Figure 78. The rules governing meetings between powerboats and other craft.

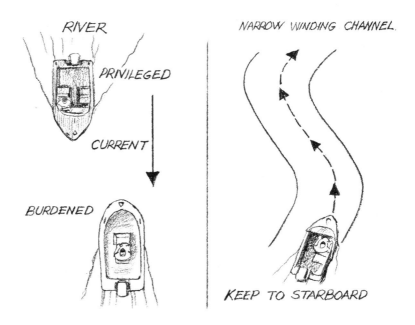

Figure 79. The rules governing movements on rivers and in narrow channels.

RULES FOR BOATS UNDER SAIL ALONE

Since it is inevitable that you will encounter sailboats when out on the water, you should also be familiar with the rules for boats under sail alone. Who knows, you may someday have both the opportunity and the desire to try your hand at sailing.

As you become familiar with these rules, you will note that they favor the boat that is sailing closehauled. That is, the privileged boat is the one that is closehauled. This ruling dates back to the days of the square-riggers, vessels that sailed poorly to windward. Sailing closehauled was thus favored by the seafaring men who originally established the rules of the road.

The rules are as follows. Whenever two sailing vessels are approaching each other in such a way that there is a risk of collision, one of the vessels must stay clear. The possible situations and the rules are: (1) *A boat that is running free will stay clear of a boat that is closehauled.* The boat running free is burdened. (2) *A boat closehauled on the port tack will stay clear of a boat closehauled on the starboard tack.* The boat on the port tack is burdened. (3) *When both boats are running free, but*

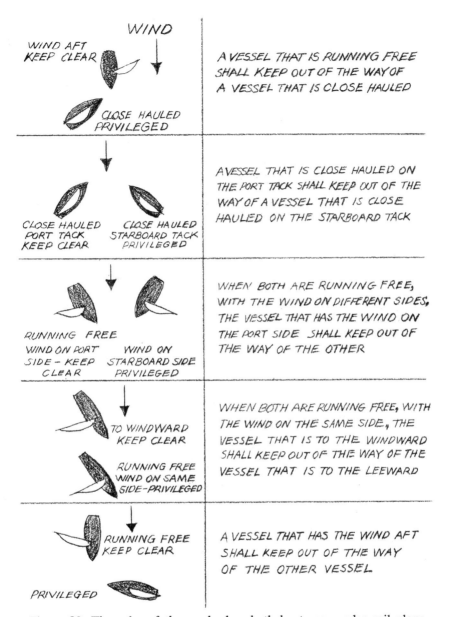

Figure 80. The rules of the road when both boats are under sail alone. Note that these rules favor the boat sailing closehauled.

with the wind on different sides, the boat that has the wind on the port side will stay clear of the other. Again, the boat on the port tack is burdened. Remember it this way: port, red, danger, burdened. (4) *When both boats are running free, with the wind on the same side, the boat that is to windward will stay clear of the boat that is to leeward.* In this case, the boat that is upwind is burdened. (5) *A boat that has the wind aft will stay clear of the other vessel.* Figure 80 illustrates these situations.

Note that the rules given here *do not apply* to sailboats in a race. The racing rules differ somewhat from the rules above, and apply only to the boats in the race; they do not apply to boats that happen onto a racing course.

It is very important that you learn these rules well and that you apply them. At the same time, keep in mind that many boatmen will not know the rules and that you will be forced to assume the responsibility for preventing accidents. By all means be upset when you observe failure to abide by the rules of the road. And you will observe such failures. We can only say that education is the answer to this type of problem. Indeed, you may find yourself in a position someday to help by participating in either the U. S. Power Squadron or Coast Guard Auxiliary safe-boating program. We hope that you will respond when the opportunity presents itself.

AIDS TO NAVIGATION

We shall briefly discuss three important *aids to navigation* in this chapter. These are *charts,* the *system of buoys* used on United States waters, and the *compass.* These three tools are indispensable to the boatman, especially the small-boat skipper who spends virtually all his time on the water near the shoreline. It is important to note that although charts, buoys, and the compass are called aids to navigation, their use in coastwise boating is called *piloting.* To be more exact, piloting is close-to-shore navigation that uses visible landmarks, sound signals, and soundings. More about basic piloting in Chapter 12. The visible landmarks used include buoys, light signals, and distinctive structures on land. For example, once a boatman becomes familiar with his home waters, he will know where he is at any given time by recognizing such structures as church steeples, water tanks, smokestacks, and unusual buildings. The sound signals all skippers become familiar with include bell, gong, and whistle buoys, and horns installed on lighthouses. A sounding is a measurement of the depth of the water. Soundings are taken to make sure there is enough water to keep the boat afloat, but also to help determine position. When a series of soundings is matched to a chart, it gives a rough approximation of position.

TABLE III

SOME IMPORTANT GOVERNMENT PUBLICATIONS

Canadian charts. Catalogues from Canadian Hydrographic Service, 249 Queen St., Ottawa, Ont., Canada.

Coast and harbor charts. National Ocean Survey, Washington, D.C. Catalogue free.

Coast Pilots. Detailed data of coastlines and entry to harbors; eight regional editions. National Ocean Survey, Washington, D.C.

Charts of the Great Lakes and connecting waters, Lake Champlain, N.Y. State Canals, Lake of the Woods, Rainy Lake. U. S. Lake Survey, 630 Federal Building, Detroit, Mich. Free catalogue.

Great Lakes Pilot. Harbor and piloting information supplemental to charts. U. S. Lake Survey.

Illinois Waterway Book of Charts. U. S. Engineer Office, Chicago, Ill.

Intracoastal waterway booklets. Data on the waterway from Norfolk, Va., to the Rio Grande. In two sections. Superintendent of Documents, Government Printing Office, Washington, D.C.

Light Lists. Characteristics of all lighted aids, in two volumes. Superintendent of Documents, Government Printing Office, Washington, D.C.

Charts of the Mississippi River. U. S. Engineer Office, 536 S. Clark St., Chicago, Ill., and Mississippi River Commission. P. O. Box 80, Vicksburg, Miss.

Charts of the Missouri River, U. S. Engineer Office, U. S. Post Office and Court House, Omaha, Nebr.

Ohio River charts. U. S. Engineer Office, P. O. Box 1159, Cincinnati, O.

Recreational Boating Guide. An eighty-page Coast Guard booklet covering equipment, numbering, buoys, safety, etc. Superintendent of Documents, Government Printing Office, Washington, D.C.

Rules of the Road and Pilot Rules, Marine Inspection. U. S. Coast Guard, Washington, D.C.

State waterways. Write for free information from individual conservation departments, care of state capitals.

Tennessee River, Kentucky Lake charts. U. S. Engineer Office, P. O. Box 1070, Nashville, Tenn.

Tide Tables; Tidal Current Tables; Current Charts. National Ocean Survey, Washington, D.C.

Western States catalogue of boating facilities entitled *Reclamation's Recreational Opportunities,* free from Department of Interior, Washington, D.C.

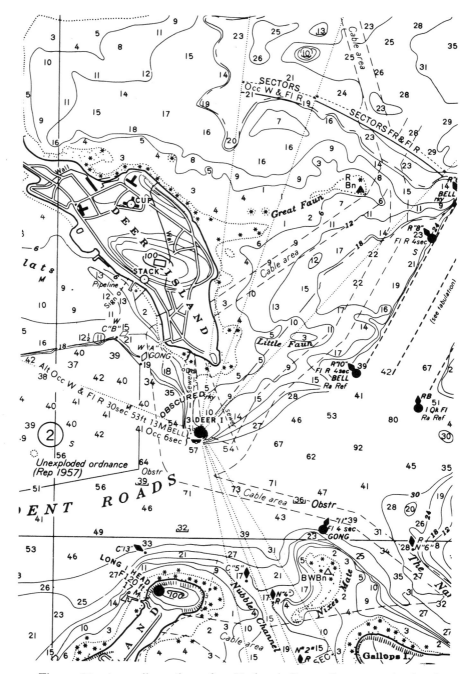

Figure 81. A small portion of a National Ocean Survey navigational chart.

CHARTS

A chart is a nautical "road map." It is easily the most important aid to navigation available to the boatman. With a chart, he can determine where he is and what the waters will hold. Without one, he might as well be blind, for he has no clue to what lies below the surface of the water. Charts of the coastal waters of the United States are published by the National Ocean Survey and distributed by the Coast Guard. Charts of the Great Lakes are available from the U. S. Lake Survey, and those for the Mississippi River are produced by the U. S. Army Corps of Engineers. For a summary of government publications, see Table III.

Figure 81 shows a small portion of a typical chart. There isn't room here to describe everything shown on charts, but we can point out a few of the more important features. The numbers shown offshore in various positions indicate the depth of the water at mean low tide. The diamond-shaped symbols next to small dots represent buoys. The solid, heavy dots represent navigational lights. For example, the lighted buoy just east of the southern tip of Deer Island is a flashing red (FL R) light. There's a good deal more to charts than this very brief introduction. When you begin boating, you should make it a point to become thoroughly familiar with the charts covering the waters you plan to use. You wouldn't think of making a long auto trip through a strange country without a road map. Be just as sensible about piloting, and always have and use the chart covering the waters you are cruising.

Another very important feature of all charts is the *compass rose*. As Figure 82 shows, the compass rose consists of two circles, each calibrated into 360 degrees. The outer circle indicates *true north,* while the inner circle shows the direction of *magnetic north.* At the center of the compass rose the *variation* is shown, as well as how much it changes annually. Variation is simply the difference between true north and magnetic north for a given area.

It's important to understand the difference between true north and magnetic north, for the compass on your boat points to magnetic north, not true north. Of course, if there are some objects containing iron near the boat's compass, its reading will be affected. This effect is called *deviation.* Correcting the deviation is important for pinpoint navigation, but it need not concern you if you make sure no tools, machinery, or a radio are stored near the compass. In practice, the boatman looks at the

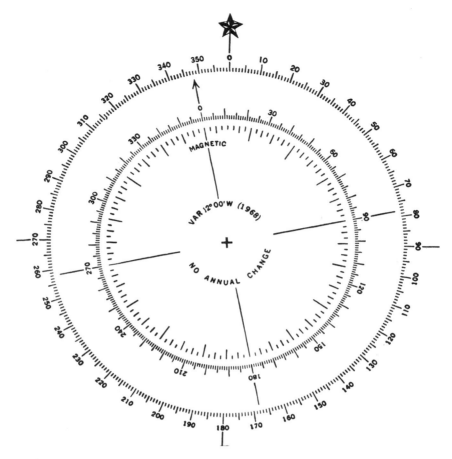

Figure 82. A typical compass rose, as seen on a chart. The inner circle shows magnetic north; these are the bearings that correspond to the readings of the boat's compass when there is no deviation.

magnetic circle of the compass rose to determine the course he must sail to reach a given destination, and then steers accordingly, using the boat's compass.

There is, of course, a great deal more to the use of charts than we have described here. A few of these skills will be presented in Chapter 12. Mastering the use of a chart is a task requiring much study and attention to detail. It is worth the effort, however, for someday a quick and accurate reading of a chart may save you from running onto a pile of rocks or aground on a sandbar.

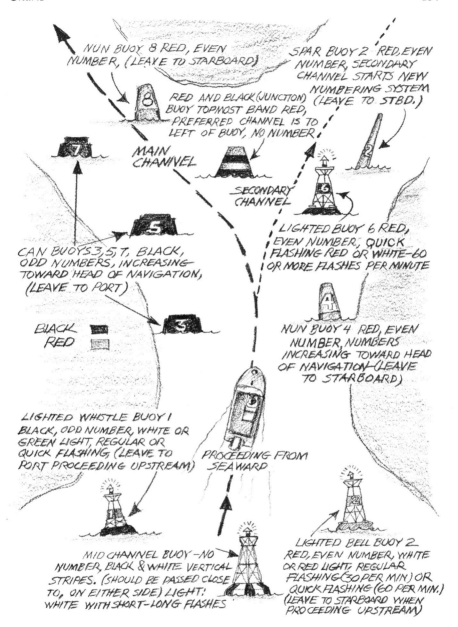

Figure 83. The buoyage system used on U.S. waters. Once you have learned the significance of the color, the shape, and the numbers used on buoys, finding your way is a relatively simple task.

BUOYS

In general, two types of buoys are in use on U.S. waters: unlighted buoys without sounds, and buoys that have sound and/or a light. Buoys are used in a systematic way that makes it very clear to a boatman where he should steer his boat. This system is based on color, buoy shape, and numbering.

Imagine you are entering a channel or harbor from seaward. See Figure 83. As you proceed up the channel, you will note the buoys on the right-hand side are red; they are also marked with even numbers. The use of *red* for buoys on the *right* side of a channel has given rise to a simple memory device: think *red, right, returning,* and you will always remember to leave the red buoys to starboard as you enter a channel, harbor, or river from seaward. Of course, when you are going toward the sea you should leave the red buoys to port.

The left-hand side of a channel when you are entering from seaward is marked by black buoys with odd numbers. Buoy shape also distinguishes the right from the left side of a channel. The red buoys on the right are conical in shape; they are called *nun* buoys. The black buoys on the left are cylindrical; they are called *can* buoys. Two other color schemes are in use. In one, black-and-white vertical stripes on an unnumbered buoy mark the middle of a channel. Boats should pass close by, but on either side of this type of buoy. In the other color scheme, black-and-red horizontal bands on a buoy indicate a channel junction or some type of underwater obstruction inside the channel itself. These buoys should be given a wide berth. They may be passed on either side, but the color of the top band indicates the preferred channel. In Figure 83, for example, the red-and-black junction buoy's top band is red. Thus the preferred channel is to the left of the buoy; the boat leaves the red top to its starboard.

Buoys that have special importance to the navigator are lighted, equipped with sound, or both. Such buoys mark the entrance to a harbor; they are used also to mark a bend in a channel. To get some idea of the importance of light and sound in buoys, just consider the following situations. You are out on open water at night and want to enter a sheltered harbor. As you approach land its mass is solid black to the eye. No landmarks are discernible. The entrance to the harbor, however, is marked by two lighted buoys. The one on the right will have either a red or a white light, with regular or quick flashing. The buoy on the left will have

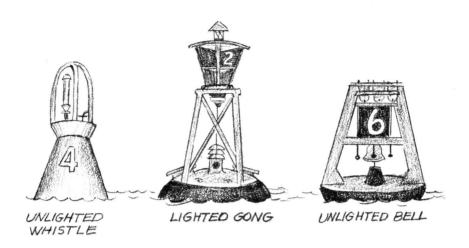

UNLIGHTED   LIGHTED GONG   UNLIGHTED BELL
WHISTLE

Figure 84. Three additional types of buoys sometimes encountered.

either a green or white light, again with regular or quick flashing. Your chart will tell you the color of the lights and also the nature of the flashing. Your job is to spot the buoys and then motor cautiously between them to enter the harbor.

In the second situation, suppose you are caught in fog, but know the general direction toward a sheltered harbor you wish to enter. Reference to your chart will tell you immediately if the harbor entrance is marked by bell or whistle buoys. With this information, you should proceed very cautiously toward the harbor entrance, following the sound of the buoys. Go very slowly and with great care in fog. You must be alert constantly to the possibility of collision. In addition, because sound behaves very strangely in fog, you must be alert to the possibility of straying away from the center of the harbor entrance.

One final comment about buoys is necessary. Every effort is made to maintain buoys in good condition and in their proper positions. This does not mean, however, that they will always be correctly placed. They may be adrift, off their charted positions because of heavy storms, unusual tides, or collisions, or even missing entirely. Because of these possibilities, a reasonable distance should always be allowed between the boat and a buoy when the buoy is passed.

Figure 85. Direct-reading compass for small- and medium-sized boats. The compass is mounted by the aluminum bracket and can be removed for safekeeping. On this instrument, adjustment screws on the bottom of the case provide a means to compensate for deviation. (*Photo courtesy of Airguide Instrument Co.*)

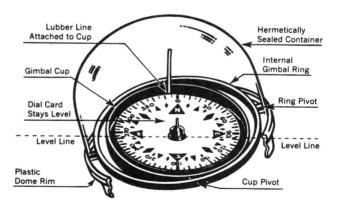

Figure 86. The structural features of an internally gimbaled compass. The compass card remains level even when the boat is pitching and rolling. (*Art courtesy of Airguide Instrument Co.*)

THE COMPASS

If your boating will never take you out of sight of familiar landmarks, you can probably do without a compass. On the other hand, if you plan to sail on large lakes, bays, or sounds, a good compass is a must. The compass should be mounted securely for easy reading by the helmsman, and away from large, iron-containing objects and electrical equipment. Always check before going out to make sure no iron or steel objects are near the compass. More than once I have discovered a sack of tools near the compass. The tools were placed there temporarily, but then forgotten. The deviation produced by such objects can greatly affect the compass reading.

Each compass has a line on its outside ring called the *lubberline.* This line indicates the heading of the boat; thus the compass must be mounted so that the lubberline and the centerline of the boat are parallel or coincide. When the compass has been installed in this position, the helmsman knows that the boat is headed in exactly the same direction as the compass reads. Of course, as you recall, this is the magnetic course, not the true course. Magnetic headings are given by the inner ring of the compass rose on a chart.

If you are really interested in mastering the art of coastwise piloting, several other aids to navigation become necessary. These include (1) *dividers,* for measuring distance on the chart; (2) *parallel rules* or a *course plotter,* for plotting or moving a course on a chart to the nearest compass rose; (3) a *pelorus,* for taking bearings; (4) a *speed indicator,* for measuring your boat's speed through the water; (5) a *lead line,* a weighted line used to measure the depth of the water; (6) *Coast Pilots,* books that give complete descriptions of ports, harbors, and coastlines; (7) *tide and current tables and charts,* and (8) *light and buoy lists.* A pair of *binoculars,* while not absolutely necessary, will often come in handy. Finally, a small *radio direction finder* (RDF) is a must if you expect to be out of sight of land. An RDF allows you to get radio bearings —that is, the direction of a radio beacon or standard broadcast station from the boat. If you know the location on a chart of two or more sending stations, getting these bearings permits you to plot your position. An RDF is an indispensable aid in fog.

12.   BASIC PILOTING

THE OUTBOARD SKIPPER interested in mastering basic piloting skills must first obtain and install on his boat the necessary tools. These include, at a minimum, charts for the waters he will be boating on, a reasonably accurate compass, dividers, a course plotter, perhaps a pelorus, and some sort of speed indicator. The average outboarder, however, faces some special problems related to using his piloting skills. To begin with, outboards lack adequate working and storage space. In addition, they tend to bounce about in the water far more than larger boats. These problems are brought into focus by imagining a skipper perched on a seat and exposed to the wind in a boat doing a lively dance, but trying at the same time to balance a chart on his lap and manipulate a pencil, course plotter, and dividers. It's a tough job, one that calls for some special adaptations.

Charts constitute the principal problem. They are large, ungainly, and extremely difficult to handle in a breeze. Sure, they can be folded up, but more often than not when you want it you'll find the chart folded out to the wrong section. Special small-craft charts, folded accordion style, have been designed to compensate for this difficulty. These charts have the letters -SC following the number in the catalog listings. Unfortunately, small-craft charts are not available for all waters, and so you often are left with the problem of what to do with large charts.

One solution is to make a loose-leaf notebook out of the chart. Cut it into pages, making sure that your vertical and horizontal cuts are parallel to the meridians of longitude and parallels of latitude spaced at equal intervals across the chart and up and down the chart. This will come in handy, as we will demonstrate shortly. Cut the necessary holes, using a preset three-hole punch, reinforce the holes with cloth rings, and insert the pages in a three-ring binder. Arrange the pagination of your chart book so that you have two-page spreads of well-traveled areas. This will mean a few odd pages at the beginning or end of your book, but since it is your creation, you should have no difficulty finding what you want.

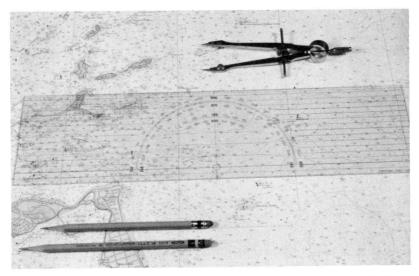

Figure 87. The tools of basic piloting. In addition to the charts, dividers, and sharp pencils shown here, you will need a compass, a speed indicator, and perhaps a pelorus.

Complete the book, if you so desire, by pasting down on each page compass roses printed on transparent plastic. This isn't really necessary, however. If you also want a mileage scale on each page, simply cut out and paste down a strip of the latitude scale from the side of the chart. More about how to use the latitude scale for mileage will be said later.

The compass on an outboard-powered boat may also present a problem. Most compasses designed for small-boat use begin to gyrate wildly just as soon as the going becomes a bit rough. Anyone who has tried it knows how difficult it is to maintain a compass heading when the compass card is whirling and dancing about. There are just two solutions to this problem. The first may be impractical: buying a compass that will remain

Figure 88. A typical pelorus. Used for taking bearings, this instrument is simply a compass card with a set of rotatable sights mounted above the card. (*Photo courtesy of Davis Instruments Corp.*)

steady in rough seas. Expense rules out this solution for most outboard skippers. The second is to adapt and make the best of existing conditions. First, slow down or stop the boat until the compass steadies, and then turn to the desired heading. At this point orient the boat's heading to a nearby object on land, a cloud formation, or to the sun's shadow across the cockpit or windshield. Hold this orientation then as you hit the throttle and accelerate to planing speeds. You'll find that you can travel a considerable distance indeed using these references before it is necessary to slow down and get another heading from the compass.

Basic piloting consists of the ability to plot courses with the use of a chart, follow plotted courses with the boat's compass, find the distance traversed for any given time under way on a course, and make a rough estimate of position at any point along a plotted course. To do all these things requires a familiarity with charts, knowledge of the effects of tidal currents, an understanding of how the compass works (including variation and deviation), and minimal skill in using the tools of the pilot. Fortunately, many of these tasks can be done at home with a chart spread out on a table. Such practice is essential if you are to react quickly and logically out on the water.

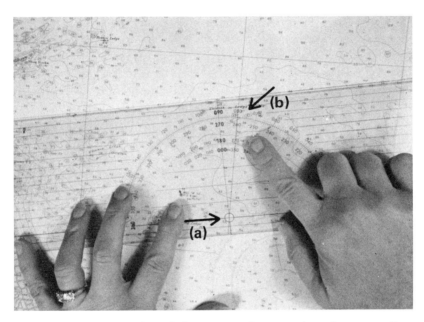

Figure 89. With the edge of the course plotter against the course line, and the bull's-eye directly over a meridian of longitude (a), the true heading of the course is read from the calibrated scale (b).

PLOTTING A COURSE

To plot a course on a chart you will need a course plotter and a pencil. We recommend a course plotter instead of parallel rules because it is easier to obtain the compass heading. The plotter illustrated here is the one used by the U. S. Power Squadrons.

First establish on the chart the *point of departure* and the *point of destination* for your trip (or segment of a trip). The straight line between these two points is the desired course. Using the edge of the plotter, draw a light, fine line between the two points. Now, with the plotter oriented as in Figure 89, place either of its long edges (or one of the ruled lines) against the course line. Slide the plotter along the course line until the center, or bull's-eye, of the calibrated scale is directly over a meridian of longitude.

If the desired direction of travel is to the right (eastward), read the *true* bearing from the top of the outer scale [Figure 90(A)]. If the course is to the left (westward), read the *true* heading from the bottom of the outer scale [Figure 90(B)]. Try this a few times, and check your headings against a nearby compass rose. A few trials will give you the hang of it. We emphasized the fact that these readings are *true* readings for a good reason. Because of magnetic variation, the compass on your boat does not give you true headings. Instead, it reads a few degrees either east or west of the true bearing; this is called the *magnetic* bearing.

Since you must steer the boat on the basis of *magnetic* bearings, it will be necessary to correct for variation. This is a simple task. Refer to the compass rose on your chart and read the variation from the center of the circle. Add westerly variation to the true reading or subtract easterly variation to obtain the magnetic bearing. For example, variation at a given location may be 015° 45′ W. To convert the true bearing to magnetic, add this value to the true reading taken off the course plotter. Suppose the plotter reads 067° for a given course. The magnetic bearing for this true reading is therefore 067° + 015° 45′ = 082° 45′. Your boat's compass should read 082° 45′; this is the heading you steer on. (You will find, however, that small-boat compasses are not calibrated to this degree of accuracy.)

Sometimes the desired course is close to north or south, and it becomes difficult to align the bull's-eye with a meridian of longitude. In these instances, the inner ring of the course plotter may be used. Simply slide the plotter along the course line until the bull's-eye is over a *parallel of latitude,* and then take the true heading off one of the two *inner scales.* As before, some practice will familiarize you with this technique.

As pointed out earlier, iron objects or electrical equipment near the compass may also affect its readings. This is called *deviation.* In this book we are assuming for the sake of simplicity that deviation is not a problem. Should it become a problem on your boat, consult the directions provided with your compass or refer the problem to an expert.

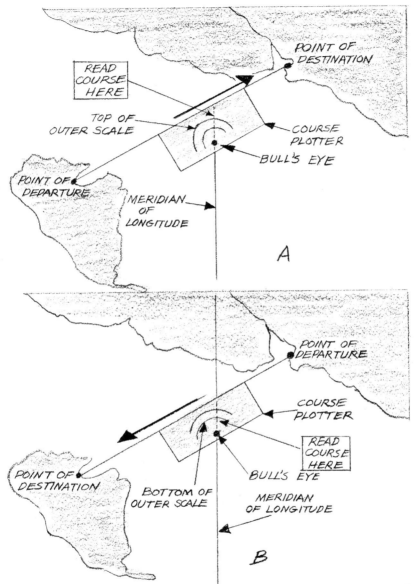

Figure 90. When plotting courses with the use of the course plotter, read true easterly headings (A) from the top of the outer scale and true westerly headings (B) from the bottom of the outer scale.

You can see now why it is important to cut the sides and bottoms of the pages in a loose-leaf chart book parallel to the meridians of longitude and parallels of latitude. When plotting a course on a "page" of the book, for example, you may not find a nearby line of longitude or latitude. If this happens, simply slide the plotter along the course line until the bull's-eye is over the side or bottom edge of the page, and then read the heading where the scale intersects the edge of the page. Purists who feel that a course should be computed to the nearest second of arc may object to this technique. We say relax and don't worry about it. For the small distances usually covered by an outboard, it takes a lot of error to make much of a difference. An error of ten degrees, for example, will set you off course only a half mile at the end of a three-mile run. It's difficult to picture errors in magnitude greater than this.

Often it is not possible to go from point of departure to point of destination in a straight line. When this is the case, a series of shorter course lines is laid out between buoys. Each of these segments, however, is treated the same as the practice courses you have been laying out. One can easily picture a course of several straight-line segments between buoys, leading through channels, around a peninsula, between islands or reefs, and so on, to a predetermined point of destination.

DETERMINING DISTANCE

Now that you have learned how to plot a course from point of departure to point of destination, the next step is to measure the distance between these points. To do this you will need a pair of dividers.

Just as on land, the basic unit of distance in use on the water is the *mile.* Boatmen, however, must contend with two types of miles. The *statute mile,* the one used for measuring land distances, is used also on inland bodies of water such as the Great Lakes and the Mississippi River. The statute mile is 5,280 feet in length. The *nautical mile,* the unit used on the high seas and connecting tidal waters, is 6,080.20 feet in length. The nautical mile is thus slightly longer than the statute mile. To convert statute miles to nautical miles, multiply by 1.15. Conversely, to convert nautical miles to statute miles it is necessary to divide by 1.15.

On the type of chart used for the high seas and connecting tidal waters, the Mercator projection, there are two scales for measuring distance. One is the latitude scale—one minute of latitude is equal to one

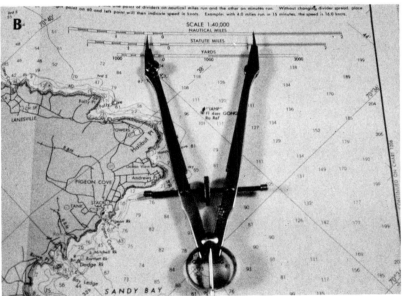

Figure 91. Measuring distance on a chart. First (A) the divider points are spread apart to the distance being measured. Then (B) without changing the spread, the dividers are transferred to the distance scale.

nautical mile. The other is a special set of distance scales found at the top and bottom of the chart. These scales usually show both nautical and statute miles.

To determine distance, place one point of the dividers on the point of departure. Then adjust the spread between the points so that the other point falls on the point of destination. You can also measure the distance between any two points this way [Figure 91(A)]. Simply transfer the dividers, without altering the spread, to the latitude scale or distance scale. If the distance scale is used as in Figure 91(B), place the dividers on the scale so that the smallest fractional units of distance can be taken from the scale.

Sometimes a course segment is so long it cannot be spanned by the dividers, even when they are opened to their full width. When this is the case, the dividers must be "walked" over the course to measure its distance. First select a convenient whole number of units from the distance scale and set the dividers to this distance. Then, starting at the point of departure, mark off this distance with the dividers, swinging them around to mark it a second time, and a third, and so on, until you reach the end of the course. Count the number of distance intervals measured and add to this total the fractional interval measured at the end of the course. For example, a given course might consist of six 4-mile intervals and one 2.5-mile interval. This course is thus 26.5 miles long.

TIME, SPEED, AND DISTANCE

Having mastered the art of plotting courses and measuring distance between two points on a chart, you will want to use these skills on the water to find out such things as:

1. How long will it take to go from point of departure to point of destination at a known speed through the water?

2. What speed must be made to travel a known distance in a given time?

3. How far will the boat go in a given time at a known speed through the water?

The additional tool needed to solve problems of this type is a speed indicator. You may be using a speedometer on your boat. If this is the case, be sure you know if the instrument is calibrated in nautical miles or statute miles, and then use the corresponding distance scale in your chart work.

A recurring problem with speedometers on small boats is reading error on the high side—the speedometer gives a speed value higher than the actual speed through the water. To check the accuracy of the speedometer on your boat, run a series of trials over a "measured mile." Measured miles are found in many localities. The mile-long course is simply two clearly visible markers exactly one nautical mile apart. You will need an accurate stopwatch to run this test.

For a reasonably accurate determination, run the course in both directions, and average the results. This will tend to cancel out the effects of wind and/or current. The procedure is quite simple. Using the stopwatch, measure the time in minutes required to traverse the mile at a fixed and uniform speed. Repeat the run in the opposite direction at the same fixed speed on the speedometer. Then, using the speed, distance, and time formula,

$$\text{SPEED IN } \frac{\text{miles}}{\text{hour}} = \frac{(1 \text{ mile}) \ (60 \text{ min/hour})}{\text{Time} \ (\text{minutes})}$$

calculate the speed for each run. Average the two speed values and then compare the result with the speedometer reading for the two runs.

Suppose, for example, that the time for run 1 is 2.45 minutes, and that the time for run 2 is 2.55 minutes. The speed for run 1 is therefore

$$S = \frac{(1 \text{ mile}) \ (60 \text{ min/hour})}{(2.45 \text{ min})}$$

$$S = 24.44 \text{ miles/hour}$$

Solving for the speed of run 2 in the same manner, the result $S = 23.56$ miles/hour is obtained. The average of these two values is then

$$\frac{24.44 + 23.56}{2} = 24.00 \text{ miles/hour}$$

But suppose you ran the two trial runs at a speedometer reading of 25 miles/hour? This tells you that in this speed range the speedometer reads about 1 mile/hour high. Thus, when doing speed, time, and distance calculations, you should use corrected speed, not the reading on the speedometer.

For those unaccustomed to or unwilling to use mathematical formulas, there are handy shortcuts to make the arithmetic easier. The "magic circle" is such a device. The magic circle for time, speed, and

distance problems is arrived at as follows. Suppose it is known that
A = BC/D. There are four values, or variables, in this formula. Now
what do you do if you wish to solve for B, or D, or C? Those familiar
with algebra will know what to do. For the rest of us, a magic circle will
work best. First, draw a circle and then divide it into quarters as shown
here:

Figure 92.

Next, label the sectors of the circle with the values from the formula
A = BC/D

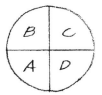

Figure 93.

The rules for using the magic circle are as follows:

1. *Division* is to be performed when the values are separated by the
horizontal line—B/A and C/D.

2. *Multiplication* is to be performed when the values are separated by
the vertical line—BC and AD.

3. The unknown being solved for must be at the bottom of the circle. If
it's at the top, simply flip the circle bottom over top.

For example, to find the value of A, cover A in the circle mentally and
perform the arithmetic remaining.

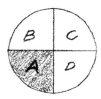

Figure 94.

A thus equals the product of B and C divided by D. A = BC/D. Using the same approach, D equals the product of B and C divided by A. D = BC/A.

To solve for B or C, first flip the circle,

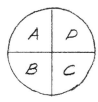

Figure 95.

then use the procedure outlined above. You should recognize immediately that B = AD/C and that C = AD/B.

The time, speed, and distance relationship is nothing more nor less than this four-part magic circle. See Figure 96.

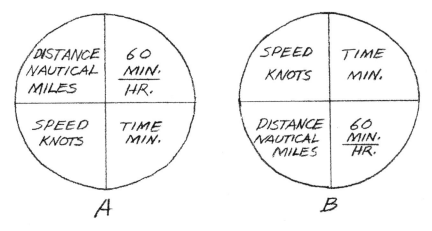

Figure 96. The "magic circle" for time, speed, and distance. Time is given in minutes, distance in nautical miles, and speed in nautical miles per hour (knots).

Now let's solve some problems like those given at the beginning of this section. Try this one first. *How long will it take to cover a course of 10 miles at a speed of 20 knots?* To solve, refer to Figure 96(A); multiply 10 miles by 60 minutes/hour and divide by 20 miles/hour. The result?

$$\frac{(10)\ (60)}{(20)} = 30 \text{ minutes.}$$

Here's another. *What will be the distance covered if a boat travels at a speed of 25 knots for 1.5 hours?* First, convert 1.5 hours to minutes: 90 minutes. Second, as shown in Figure 96(B), multiply 25 miles/hour by 90 minutes and divide by 60 minutes/hour. The result?

$$\frac{(25)\ (90)}{60} = 37.5 \text{ miles.}$$

Last, but not least, try this one. *A boat travels 22 miles in three quarters of an hour. What was its average speed through the water?* First, convert three quarters of an hour to minutes: 45 minutes. Second, using Figure 96(A), multiply 22 miles by 60 minutes/hour and divide by 45 minutes. Here's how it comes out.

$$\frac{(22)\ (60)}{45} = 29.44 \text{ miles/hour (knots).}$$

Clearly, it is not possible to master the use of time, speed, and distance calculations by mentally running through a few samples. Only practice, both over a spread-out chart on the dining room table and out on your boat, will lead to mastery of this skill. For reasons that will be developed a bit later, you will see that it is a skill that may come in very handy some day.

PLOTTING BEARINGS AND FIXES

The purpose behind plotting bearings is to determine position. A bearing is simply the direction of an object, or landmark, from the person looking —in this case, you, the skipper of an outboard-powered boat. For coastwise piloting purposes, the objects sighted on are fixed in position. Gas tanks, lighthouses, distinctive towers, flagpoles, and other objects marked on the chart are typical examples. Suppose you are running a long course parallel to a shoreline and wish to know how much progress you have made. That is, you wish to know where you are. By taking and plotting two or more bearings you will have made a "fix" of the boat's approximate position along the plotted course. Thus, in addition to knowing how to plot courses and find time, speed, and distance over plotted courses, this skill enables you to approximate the position of your boat at any point along a course. It is not necessary, however, to be under way on a plotted course to determine rough position by taking bearings. Your boat may be at anchor, or it may be drifting—during a fishing trip, for example, or perhaps (let us hope not) because you are out of fuel!

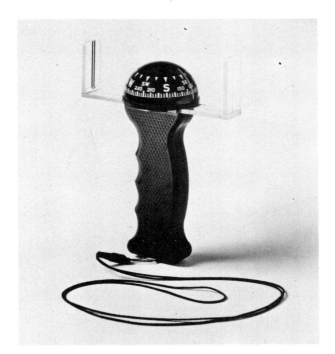

Figure 97. A hand-bearing compass such as this one is useful for taking bearings as well as for steering the boat. (*Photo courtesy of Davis Instruments Corp.*)

The skipper of a small boat has a choice of methods for taking bearings. The simplest of these methods is to use the boat's compass while it is mounted in position. Slow the boat down until the compass steadies, and then point the boat at the landmark chosen for the bearing. With the boat's heading steady on the landmark, take down the compass reading. This is the bearing from the boat to the object sighted on.

Some small-boat compasses, on the other hand, are designed to be easily unshipped from their mountings. These compasses, when dismounted, can be hand held at eye level to take bearings. It is a simple matter to hold the lubberline of the compass along the centerline of the boat and read the bearing of the landmark by sighting across the compass. Keep in mind, however, when using this technique that the compass should be kept away from iron-containing or electrical devices. Note also that, because the compass is hand held, bearings obtained by this method are rough approximations only.

A more versatile instrument for taking bearings is the pelorus. See Figure 88. A pelorus is simply a compass card with a set of rotatable sights

Figure 98. A portable RDF with the sights on the rotating antenna elevated; when set up this way the instrument can be used as a pelorus to take bearings.

mounted above the card. The simplest way to use the pelorus is to place the instrument so that 000° is dead ahead, that is, along or parallel to the centerline of the boat. With the instrument in position, the rotating sights are then used to measure the direction of the landmark. Bearings obtained this way are called *relative bearings*. They must be converted to compass bearings by adding the heading of the boat as read from the boat's steering compass. For example, suppose the boat's heading is 030° magnetic (that is, including the effect of variation), and that a water tower is determined to be 040° off the starboard bow. The compass bearing of the tower is therefore 070° (030° + 040°) magnetic from the boat. If the sum of the boat's heading and the bearing of the landmark is greater than 360°, simply subtract 360° to obtain the correct bearing.

Many portable direction finders can also be used as a pelorus. See Figure 98. In use, the case of the instrument is set up at right angles (athwartships) to the centerline of the boat. This places the 000° heading of the calibrated scale dead ahead. To take a bearing, the navigator simply rotates the antenna to line up the landmark in the sights. He then reads the relative bearing from the scale on top of the instrument case. The use of an RDF in plotting fixes by means of radio bearings will be discussed shortly.

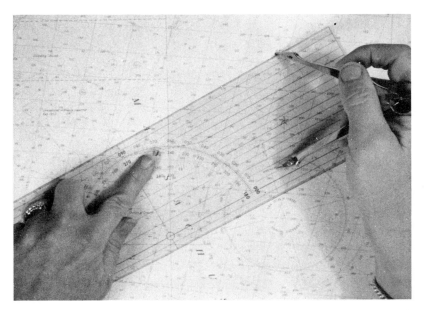

Figure 99. Plotting a bearing. With a point of the dividers on the land-mark and the bull's-eye over a meridian of longitude, the plotter is moved up or down until the desired bearing on the scale appears over the line of longitude. The bearing line is then drawn.

To plot a fix on a chart, it is necessary first to be able to plot bearings. This is similar to laying a course, and is done the same way for both visual bearings and radio bearings taken with an RDF. The course plotter, a pair of dividers, a sharp pencil, and of course the proper chart are used to plot bearings.

First the bearings must be known. Moreover, if the bearing includes the affect of variation, it must be corrected. As mentioned earlier, this is readily done. Since a true bearing is converted to a magnetic bearing by adding westerly variation, the reverse is accomplished by subtracting westerly variation. Similarly, converting a magnetic bearing to true bearing when the variation is easterly requires that the variation be added to the magnetic bearing.

Once the true bearing has been computed, it is easily plotted. First, the navigator places a point of the dividers on the landmark—the object on which the bearing was taken. Then he places the edge of the course plotter against the divider point, with the bull's-eye of the plotter over a meridian of longitude. See Figure 99. Now, keeping the edge of the plotter against the divider point and the bull's-eye over the meridian, he moves the plotter up or down until the desired bearing on the scale inter-

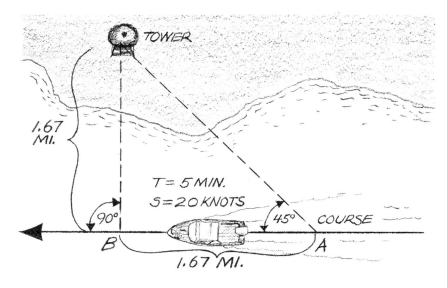

Figure 100. The bow-and-beam bearing. With speed known and the time of passage measured, the distance between the two bearings A and B is the same as the distance between the boat and the tower at the point of bearing B.

sects the meridian. At this point he draws the bearing line on the chart. As noted before, he uses the two outer scales on the plotter when the bull's-eye is aligned over a meridian of longitude. He uses the inner scales when the bearing line is very close to north or south and the navigator elects to center the bull's-eye over a parallel of latitude.

Plotting a fix is a simple task once you have acquired the ability to plot bearings. First, the bearings are converted to *lines of position*. A line of position (LOP) is the reciprocal of a bearing. That is, an LOP is 180° away from a bearing. Suppose, for example, that you locate a lighthouse on a point of land bearing 120° true from the bow. You are therefore somewhere on a line 300° from the lighthouse. The line drawn on the chart at 300° true from the lighthouse is a line of position. When two or more lines of position are drawn on a chart, the point where they intersect or converge is your approximate position. Don't make the mistake of assuming that chart fixes are precise. Most often you will find that they are just good approximations of positions, at best.

Sometimes you will find only one identifiable landmark ahead on which to take bearings. If you are following a plotted course at known speed, and will leave the landmark either to port or starboard as you pass, it is possible to determine your position by taking two successive bearings. This is called a bow-and-beam bearing. The first bearing is taken, and the time noted, when the landmark is 045° from the bow. The time is then noted again when the landmark bears 090° from the bow (abeam). With both the speed of the boat and the elapsed time known, the distance the boat traveled between bearings is easily computed. But, because of the geometry of the triangle, the distance between the boat and the landmark when the landmark bears 090° is the same as the distance traveled between the bearings. Consider the example shown in Figure 100. A boat is following the course shown at a fixed speed of 20 knots, and will leave the tower to starboard. The bow-and-beam bearings on the flagpole are taken, and the time between bearings noted to be 5 minutes exactly. Using the magic circle for speed, time, and distance,

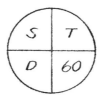

Figure 101.

the distance traveled between bearings is computed to be

$$D = \frac{(S)\ (T)}{(60)} = \frac{(20)\ (5)}{(60)} = 1.67 \text{ miles}$$

The boat is therefore 1.67 miles away from the flagpole when the flagpole is directly abeam (at 090° to the boat's course). Thus, by taking two bearings on a single object when speed is known, and by noting the time between the bearings, it is possible to determine the position of the boat. Again, however, remember that, as useful as this technique may seem, it gives only a rough approximation of position.

FINDING LATITUDE AND LONGITUDE

To find position, the navigator plots two or more bearings. The approximate position of the boat is then where the bearings intersect or converge. With the shoreline in sight and a chart spread out before him,

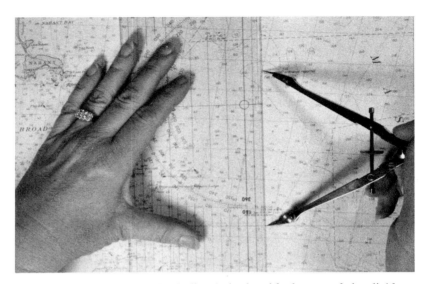

Figure 102. The first step in finding latitude with the use of the dividers.
With the plotter aligned parallel to a meridian of longitude, the dividers
are used to measure the distance between the boat and the parallel of
latitude below it on the chart.

the skipper can speak confidently about his location. Suppose, however,
that he is some distance offshore, or in unfamiliar waters, and wishes to
inform another boat by radio of his whereabouts. Suppose also that he
has plotted a fix visually, using a couple of buoys or perhaps a lightship,
or that he has made a fix using the RDF. Pick a point well offshore on a
chart and ask yourself how you would tell another skipper where you are.
Of the several possible ways to do this, the simplest is to pinpoint your
position by latitude and longitude.

Finding latitude and longitude on a chart is a relatively simple task.
You will need the course plotter and a pair of dividers. To find latitude,
first place the edge of the course plotter on the point of position of the
boat. Then, keeping the plotter's edge parallel to a meridian of longitude, measure with the dividers the distance between the boat's position
and the parallel of latitude below it on the chart. To read the latitude
value, transfer the dividers to the edge of the chart and read from the
scale provided. This procedure is shown in Figures 102 and 103.

The longitude value of the boat's position is obtained by the same
method. In this case, however, the edge of the course plotter is kept parallel to a parallel of latitude, and the distance from the nearest meridian of

Figure 103. The second step in finding latitude using the dividers. Without changing the spread of the dividers, they are transferred to the edge of the chart to read the position.

longitude to the boat's position is measured. The dividers are then transferred to the top or bottom of the chart to make the reading. Position is thus given as the intersection of an imaginary meridian of longitude and an imaginary parallel of latitude.

THE RADIO DIRECTION FINDER (RDF)

A portable radio direction finder is the only simple and inexpensive radio aid to navigation available to the small-boat operator. Many of these instruments serve an entertainment function—they receive standard broadcast frequencies. In addition, of course, they receive the radio beacon frequencies used for navigation. A typical modern RDF is shown in Figure 104. To the operator of an outboard, the RDF is primarily a safety device. It will in all probability be used only rarely for anything other than entertainment. Should the need arise, however, this versatile instrument can be used to find position, steer a course by "homing" on a known radio beacon or broadcast station, or determine distance from a *distance-finding station* (DFS).

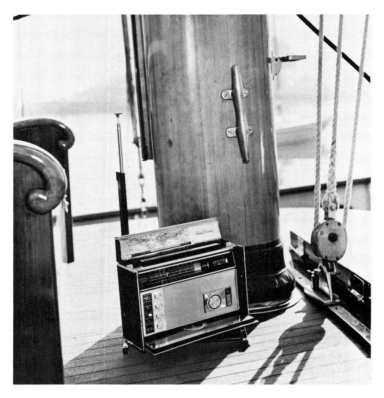

Figure 104. A modern portable RDF mounted on a swivel base to permit radio direction finding. (*Photo courtesy of Zenith Radio Corp.*)

In use, the radio direction finding system consists of (1) one or more
radio beacon transmitters at known locations (both seacoasts, the Great
Lakes, and other large inland bodies of water have numerous transmitters; radio beacon charts are published in *Light Lists*); (2) an RDF on
board the boat; (3) charts covering both the locations of the radio beacon
transmitters and the waters the boat is operating on; and (4) an operator
who understands how to use the system.

The key feature of an RDF is the directional antenna. This is the
rectangular rotating object mounted on top of the sets illustrated in this
chapter, except for the set shown in Figure 104, on which the entire set
rotates on a fixed swivel base. As you saw in Figure 98, the rotating
antenna may carry sights to permit use of the instrument as a pelorus.
When used for radio direction finding, the rotating antenna has maximum

pickup strength—reception is loudest—when the broad side of the antenna faces the incoming signal. The reception is therefore weakest when either end of the antenna faces the transmitter.

To take a bearing on a transmitter, the navigator mounts the instrument with its base athwartships (at right angles to the centerline of the boat). He then tunes the set to the desired frequency and rotates the antenna until the signal is weakest. The antenna is now pointing directly at the transmitting station; the navigator then reads the bearing from the scale mounted on the set. If two or more such bearings are taken and plotted, the intersection of the lines of position gives the boat's approximate location.

DEAD RECKONING

Originally "deduced" reckoning, then "ded" reckoning, and finally "dead" reckoning (DR), this technique is the process of determining a boat's approximate position by using the courses and speeds sailed from the last well-established position. Because there will always be times when it is impossible to determine position accurately—at night, in a fog, or when buoys have been lost in a storm, for example—the outboard skipper should have the skill needed to determine his most probable position. This calls for a working knowledge of everything that has been covered in this chapter.

The basic elements of dead reckoning for the small-boat skipper are these: (1) magnetic courses only are plotted; (2) speed and therefore distance must be measurable; (3) a DR plot is always plotted from a previously known position; and (4) the effects of current are always ignored.

In simpler language, this means that the skipper uses his piloting skills and tools to keep a chart record of where he is going, but always from the last-known position. A DR plot may include several course lines before another known position is established. Thus, to be as accurate as possible, a DR position should be plotted (1) at every course change; (2) at every speed change; (3) every hour on the hour; and (4) at the time of every fix.

It isn't possible in this book to give any more space to dead reckoning. This should not, however, be construed as evidence that dead reckoning is unimportant. Nothing could be farther from the truth. Maintaining DR plots is much more than an interesting technique for determining approximate position. It leads also to another skill that, for want of a better term, is best called "mental" dead reckoning.

Just what is mental dead reckoning? This is a skill that makes the most of observation and memory. If it is inconvenient or impossible to maintain a DR plot on a chart, the skipper observes and notes such conditions as cloud formations, wind direction, the movement of wave patterns, and any changes in these phenomena that may take place. With a picture of these factors in mind, plus the memory of courses taken and distances covered, the skipper has a mental DR position at all times. Many's the seawise boatman who, though apparently lost, has found his way home using mental dead reckoning. It's a skill well worth acquiring.

It should be noted that the introduction to piloting presented in this chapter is just that—an introduction. It is intended to get you started, perhaps to give you enough skill to help you find your way home in a tight spot, but nothing more. You should follow up on this meager beginning and acquire a real competence in the skills of the pilot. There are many ways to do this, but perhaps the best is to enroll in the appropriate U. S. Power Squadron or Coast Guard Auxiliary courses. This effort will be repaid many times over in terms of safety and enjoyment while you are on the water.

13. SAFETY AND COURTESY
AFLOAT

WHENEVER WE READ or hear of a tragic accident that has taken place on the water, there is a tendency to think that it can't happen to us. Nothing could be farther from the truth. Accidents show no preference, unless it is to the habitually careless boatman. The careful boatman, on the other hand, can look forward to happy and rewarding hours on the water, because he has made it a habit to prevent potential accidents before they have a chance to develop. This is the crux of the matter. Boating, like other active sports, is not completely free of danger. It is, however, a sport whose dangerous elements can be controlled. The secret is to anticipate what might happen and then to take preventive steps. This doesn't mean that you should be overly cautious. It does mean, however, that you should understand the capabilities of your boat, the sea and weather conditions you can expect to face, and yourself.

SAFETY EQUIPMENT

Throughout this book we have stressed safe boating practices as well as the equipment needed to assure safety. At this point we want to bring the question of safety to a focus and review the essential safety equipment for outboard-powered craft. Keep in mind that the Coast Guard may not require all the items we will list. Its requirements are the legal limits only. The prudent boatman will supplement the required equipment with enough additional equipment to handle whatever conditions the boat and crew can expect to meet.

Figure 105. The action is fast, wet, and wonderful, but safety standards must be adhered to rigorously to keep it that way. (*Photo courtesy of Johnson Motors.*)

To begin with, for boats less than 16 feet in length the Coast Guard now requires one approved wearable life preserver (now called a PFD —*personal flotation device*) or a buoyant cushion for each person on board. For boats 16 feet or greater in length, there must be an approved wearable life jacket for each person aboard plus at least one throwable device—a buoyant cushion or ring buoy. Moreover, all persons on the boat should be instructed in the use of life preservers. At least one adequately heavy anchor plus enough anchor line is a must also. Be sure to include a bilge pump or bucket for bailing; you never know when your boat may leak, ship water from spray or high waves, or capsize. A sponge or absorbent rag is handy for completely drying the bilge. Be sure to carry a pair of paddles or oars just in case the engine should quit.

It's wise to carry some tools and spare parts. A good knife, a pair of pliers, and a screwdriver are essential. Better yet, carry a tool kit properly

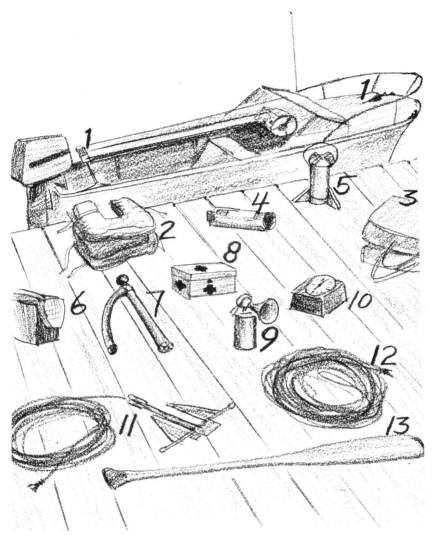

Figure 106. The safety and emergency equipment either required or recommended for small boats: (1) running lights, (2) life jackets or (3) buoyant seat cushions for all hands, (4) fire extinguisher, (5) distress signal kit, (6) flashlight, (7) bilge pump, (8) first-aid kit, (9) air horn, (10) compass, (11) anchor and line, (12) at least fifty feet of extra line, and (13) paddle or pair of oars.

equipped for trouble-shooting engine problems. Be sure also to take along spare spark plugs and extra shear pins for the propeller.

You should always carry a horn or whistle, adequate docking lines, a chart of the waters you are cruising, and a compass if you plan to go off-shore. Despite the fact that you may never use it, a first-aid kit is essen-

TABLE IV—EQUIPMENT REQUIREMENTS

MINIMUM REQUIRED EQUIPMENT

EQUIPMENT	CLASS A (Less than 16 feet)	CLASS 1 (16 feet to less than 26 feet)	CLASS 2 (26 feet to less than 40 feet)	CLASS 3 (40 feet to not more than 65 feet)
BACK-FIRE FLAME ARRESTOR	One approved device on each carburetor of all gasoline engines installed after April 25, 1940, except outboard motors.			
VENTILATION	At least two ventilator ducts fitted with cowls or their equivalent for the purpose of properly and efficiently ventilating the bilges of every engine and fuel-tank compartment of boats constructed or decked over after April 25, 1940, using gasoline or other fuel of a flashpoint less than 110° F.			
BELL	None.*	None.*	One, which when struck, produces a clear, bell-like tone of full round characteristics.	
LIFE-SAVING DEVICES	One approved buoyant cushion or wearable life preserver for each person on board.	One approved wearable life preserver for each person on board plus at least one approved throwable device—buoyant cushion or ring buoy—on the boat.		

TABLE IV—EQUIPMENT REQUIREMENTS (cont'd.)

WHISTLE	None.*	One hand, mouth, or power-operated, audible at least ½ mile.	One hand or power-operated, audible at least 1 mile.	One power-operated, audible at least 1 mile.
FIRE EXTINGUISHER— PORTABLE† When *no fixed* fire extinguishing system is installed in machinery space(s).	At least One B-1 type approved hand portable fire extinguisher. (Not required on outboard motorboat less than 26 feet in length and not carrying passengers for hire if the construction of such motorboats will not permit the entrapment of explosive or flammable gases or vapors.)	At least two B-1 type approved hand portable fire extinguishers; *or* at least one B–11 type approved hand portable fire extinguisher.	At least two B-1 type approved hand portable fire extinguishers; *or* at least one B–11 type approved hand portable fire extinguisher.	At least two B-1 type approved hand portable fire extinguishers; *or* at least one B–11 type approved hand portable fire extinguisher.
When fixed fire extinguishing system is installed in machinery space(s).	None.	None.	At least one B-1 type approved hand portable fire extinguisher.	At least three B-1 type approved hand portable fire extinguishers; *or* at least one B–11 type approved hand portable fire extinguisher.

Fire extinguishers manufactured after Janurary 1, 1965 will be marked, "Marine Type USCG Type _____ Size _____ Approval No. 162–028. . . ."

* Not required by the Motorboat Act of 1940; however, the "rules of the road" require these vessels to sound proper signals.
† Toxic vaporizing-liquid type fire extinguishers, such as those containing carbon tetrachloride or chlorobromomethane, are not accepted as required approved extinguishers on uninspected vessels (private pleasure craft).

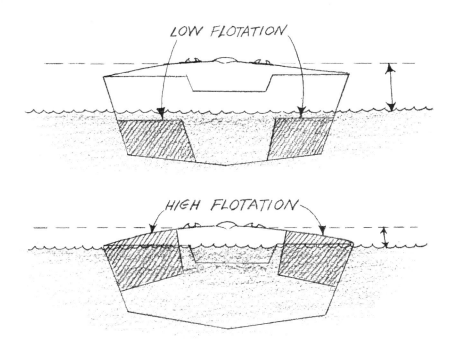

Figure 107. Flotation tanks placed high in a hull give more stability when the boat has been swamped.

tial. Remember, however, to replace and refresh the contents of the first-aid kit periodically. Carry a flashlight at all times; you never know when you'll be delayed and have to make it into home port after dark. Of course, if you intend to do any boating at night, full navigation lights are required. Finally, carry extra line, a boat hook, fenders, waterproof tape for quick repairs, and a small can of lubricating oil.

All the safety and emergency equipment mentioned here is shown in Figure 106. Some of these items, while recommended, are not required. Table IV, on the other hand, gives the minimum safety equipment required by the Coast Guard for the different classes of boats.

With respect to the safe operation of pleasure boats, the Federal Boat Safety Act of 1971 contains a passage of great significance for the owners and operators of all boats. It is quoted here without change, with the added note that the Coast Guard has made it clear that it intends to enforce the law. The wise skipper will heed this advice.

If a Coast Guard boarding officer observes a boat being used without sufficient lifesaving or firefighting devices or in an overloaded or other unsafe condition as defined in regulations of the Secretary, and in his judgment such use creates an especially hazardous condition, he

Figure 108. The ultimate in flotation. Even when swamped and loaded as shown here, this utility runabout is stable and unsinkable. Very few boats can boast of this capability, although perhaps they all should be able to. (*Photo courtesy of Dell Quay Marine, Ltd.*)

may direct the operator to take whatever immediate and reasonable steps would be necessary for the safety of those aboard the vessel, including directing the operator to return to mooring and to remain there until the situation creating the hazard is corrected or ended.

Safe operation requires an understanding of the type of flotation used on your boat, if in fact your boat carries any flotation at all. Aluminum and Fiberglas boats will sink if they are flooded, unless flotation has been installed. Wooden boats will usually float when swamped, although sometimes the weight of the engine is enough to sink a swamped wooden boat. As Figure 107 shows, flotation tanks can be placed so that the boat will float either high or low when swamped. Low flotation tanks will often keep the water level low within the boat, but the boat will be somewhat unstable; it may turn turtle when capsized. When the flotation tanks are placed high, the boat rides very low in the water. As a result it is more stable.

NUMBERING

The Federal Boating Act of 1958 establishes a uniform system for the identification of pleasure craft. Undocumented vessels are to be numbered by the state in which the boat is principally used. If a boat is propelled by machinery of over ten horsepower, and is used principally on navigable waters of the United States in New Hampshire, Washington, Alaska, the District of Columbia, or Guam, the Certificate of Number will be issued by the Coast Guard. When a vessel is used principally on the high seas, it is to be numbered in the state in which it is usually docked, moored, housed, or garaged. The identification number issued to a vessel is shown on the Certificate of Number. With each certificate issued by the Coast Guard, two color-coded validation stickers will also be issued. The Certificate of Number must be on board whenever the vessel is in operation.

A number awarded by the Coast Guard is valid for three years from the date of the owner's birthday next occurring after the certificate is issued, and must be renewed before the expiration date. Renewal applications are mailed to applicants ninety days before expiration. If not renewed within one year after expiration date, the number will be voided and a new number may be assigned at later application.

The identification number should be painted on or attached to each side of the forward half of the vessel (the bow); no other number may be displayed. Numbers are to read left to right, be in block characters, be of a color contrasting with the background, and be not less than three inches in height. There shall be a hyphen or space between the prefix letters and numerals and between the numerals and suffix letters. The hyphen or space shall be equal to the width of any letter except "I" or any number except "1." The validation sticker must be placed three inches beyond, and level with, the last letter of the identification number.

States other than those mentioned above have their own federally conforming boat registration laws. State fees are fixed by state law. A number issued by a state may be valid for not more than three years. The state may require the numbering of vessels carrying less than ten horsepower.

Information about state numbering systems is available from state agencies, Coast Guard units, and marine dealers. Each state with an approved numbering system must recognize for a period of at least ninety days the validity of a number issued by the Coast Guard or by another state having an approved system.

ANCHOR LIGHTS AND RUNNING LIGHTS

Most outboard skippers confine their boating activities to the daylight hours. Some, however, will want to use their boats at night. Others, because of circumstances they can't control, will find themselves away from home port at night. Because of the likelihood that sooner or later you will be out in your boat at night, it is important that you understand the purpose and function of both the anchor light and running lights. Lights are carried on boats between sundown and sunrise to show their presence to other boats. To be more specific, running lights indicate the approximate size of a boat and its approximate heading. An anchor light shows the presence of a boat and tells other skippers that the boat is at anchor.

Anchor and running lights are defined and described in terms of color and *arc of visibility*. The point system is used to describe arc of visibility. One point equals 11.25 degrees. Thus, thirty-two points equals a full 360 degrees. A thirty-two-point light is visible to another boat from all directions. All lights except the red and green sidelights or combination lights are white.

The direction of travel of a boat is shown by the sidelights or combination lights. Facing forward, the light on the boat's port (left) side is red; the starboard light is green. Each of these lights is to be visible over an arc of ten points, from dead ahead to two points abaft (behind) the beam. If, for example, when traveling at night, another boat appears off your starboard bow (in the danger zone) and you see a green running light only, you know the other boat is going in the opposite direction. He will probably pass to your starboard. If the other boat shows a red light, however, he is going in the same direction as your boat, and collision is a possibility. If you see red and green at the same time, you know the other boat is headed toward you on what may very well be a collision course.

Different combinations of running lights are required for different running conditions by different types of vessels. By far the most important of these differences is the one between a boat under power and a sailboat under sail alone. See Figure 111. A sailboat under sail alone carries a twelve-point white light at the stern. No white light shows forward on a sailboat under sail alone. All craft under power (including sailboats under *sail and power*), however, show a full thirty-two-point white light. See Figure 112 for one such arrangement. Under the international rules, there are some lighting options available. These are shown in Figure 110.

Under certain circumstances an anchored boat must show its presence

INLAND RULES

THESE LIGHTS MAY BE SHOWN ONLY ON INLAND WATERS

		UNDER 26 FT.	26 FT. OR OVER NOT MORE THAN 65 FT.
INBOARDS, OUTBOARDS OR AUXILIARIES	POWER ALONE	WHITE ALL AROUND (32 PT) 2 MI. — COMBINATION RED & GREEN 20 PT. 1 MI.	WHITE ALL AROUND (32 PT) 2 MI. — SEPARATE SIDELIGHTS 10 PT. 1 MI. — WHITE 20 PT. 2 MI.
	SAIL & POWER	COMBINATION RED & GREEN 20 PT. 1 MI. — WHITE ALL AROUND (32 PT) 2 MI.	WHITE ALL AROUND (32 PT) 2 MI. — WHITE 20 PT. 2 MI. — SEPARATE SIDELIGHTS 10 PT. 1 MI.
	SAIL ALONE	WHITE 12-PT. STERN LIGHT 2 MI. — COMBINATION RED AND GREEN 20 PT. 1 MI.	WHITE 12-PT. STERN LIGHT 2 MI. — SEPARATE SIDELIGHTS 10 PT. 1 MI.

MANUALLY PROPELLED VESSELS SHALL HAVE READY AT HAND A LANTERN SHOWING A WHITE LIGHT WHICH SHALL BE TEMPORARILY EXHIBITED IN SUFFICIENT TIME TO PREVENT COLLISION

Figure 109.

INTERNATIONAL RULES

LIGHTS UNDER INTERNATIONAL RULES MAY BE SHOWN ON INLAND WATERS AND ARE REQUIRED ON THE HIGH SEAS

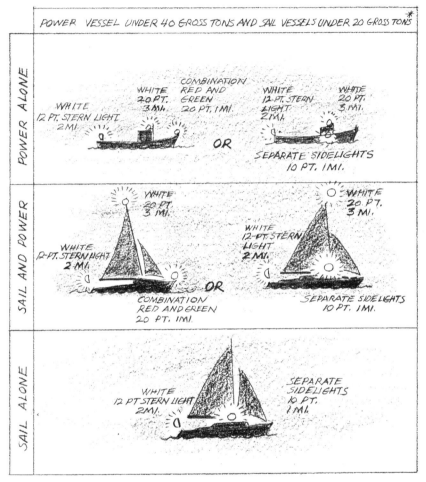

POWER VESSEL UNDER 40 GROSS TONS AND SAIL VESSELS UNDER 20 GROSS TONS

POWER ALONE

WHITE 12 PT. STERN LIGHT 2 MI.

WHITE 20 PT. 3 MI.

COMBINATION RED AND GREEN 20 PT. 1 MI.

OR

WHITE 12 PT. STERN LIGHT 2 MI.

WHITE 20 PT. 3 MI.

SEPARATE SIDELIGHTS 10 PT. 1 MI.

SAIL AND POWER

WHITE 20 PT. 3 MI.

WHITE 12 PT. STERN LIGHT 2 MI.

OR

COMBINATION RED AND GREEN 20 PT. 1 MI.

WHITE 20 PT. 3 MI.

WHITE 12 PT. STERN LIGHT 2 MI.

SEPARATE SIDELIGHTS 10 PT. 1 MI.

SAIL ALONE

WHITE 12 PT STERN LIGHT 2 MI.

SEPARATE SIDELIGHTS 10 PT. 1 MI.

* UNDER INTERNATIONAL RULES POWERBOATS OF 40 GROSS TONS OR OVER MUST CARRY SEPARATE SIDELIGHTS, VISIBLE 2 MILES, AND A 20-POINT WHITE LIGHT, VISIBLE 5 MILES. SAILING VESSELS OF 20 GROSS TONS OR OVER MUST CARRY SEPARATE SIDELIGHTS, VISIBLE 2 MILES. UNDER SAIL, ONLY BOATS OF LESS THAN 20 TONS MAY USE A COMBINATION.

Figure 110.

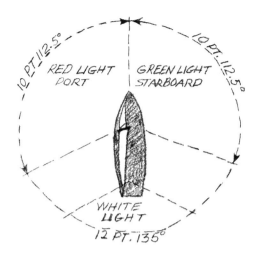

Figure 111. Running lights for a sailboat under twenty-six feet in length operating under sail alone. Separate port and starboard lights are permissible also.

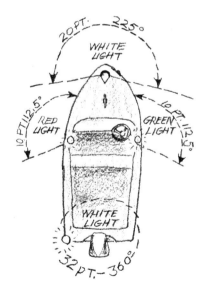

Figure 112. The required running lights for a boat twenty-six feet or more in length operating under power.

by displaying an *anchor light.* If you drop the hook in an area designated on a chart as a special anchorage area, no anchor light is required. If you anchor anywhere else, however, you must show a white thirty-two-point light on the forward part of your boat no higher than twenty feet above the deck. To be on the safe side, many cruising skippers display an anchor light even when they drop the hook in a special anchorage area. Anchor lights must remain lit from sundown to sunrise.

One final word about lights. No bright lights other than a boat's running lights should be visible at night. Other lights create additional confusion under circumstances that are difficult at best anyway. Powerful spot-lights, in particular, should be avoided. Unless absolutely essential, as when you are entering a strange port and it is necessary to illuminate and identify buoys, a searchlight or spotlight should never be used above decks. And most important of all, never train a spotlight on another boat. You run the risk of temporarily blinding the helmsman, a severe handicap indeed when running at night.

MAN OVERBOARD!

Despite every effort to prevent it from happening, people do fall out of or are knocked off boats. In calm weather, this is seldom a problem. It can be a serious problem in rough weather, however, for the boat may be difficult to maneuver and thus may injure the person in the water. There is a definite procedure to follow when someone falls off your boat. Learn it thoroughly, and you will save yourself a lot of trouble when you have to pick somebody out of the water. The first thing to do when somebody goes overboard is to stop the boat and then make sure the victim has a life jacket. If he isn't wearing one, throw him one immediately. Next, have a member of the crew get the person overboard in his sight; *until the pickup, he should not take his eyes off the victim,* regardless of the maneuvering necessary to bring the boat alongside.

To pick up the victim, make your approach as you would to a mooring. Come in slowly, and slightly to windward. Shut off the engine when you are within a few feet of the victim, but stay far enough away during the pickup so that the hull cannot strike him. In very rough weather, try to get a line to the victim rather than attempt to have him catch hold of a heaving hull. To a person in the water, a violently heaving boat can be a lethal weapon. During the actual pickup the engine should be shut off. There are two reasons for this precaution. First, even when the gearshift is in neutral the propeller can spin fast enough to cause injury. Second, there is always the possibility that someone will accidentally knock the engine into gear during the confusion of bringing the victim aboard.

Under no circumstances should anyone ever attempt to climb aboard a boat using the cavitation plate on the engine's lower unit as a step. Time and time again very serious injuries have resulted from falls against the sharp protruding edges of the lower unit. Use a boarding ladder, handholds, or steps attached to the transom, or lift the victim from the water.

If it should be your misfortune to go overboard someday, the first thing to do is keep calm. Stay afloat the easiest way you can—put on or hang onto the life jacket thrown to you. Don't tire yourself by trying to swim to the boat. Let it come to you. As it approaches, watch carefully, and if it appears to be coming too close, use your strength to swim clear. Then, after you have caught hold of the gunwale of the boat, or a line, climb back aboard. Dry yourself quickly and put on warm clothes to avoid catching cold.

DROWNPROOFING

The great majority of drownings associated with boating accidents need not occur. Too often boatmen thrown into the water forget or refuse to stay with the boat. In addition, many have never attempted to learn how to stay afloat fully clothed, or even how to disrobe in the water. These are important, of course, because boatmen often wear bulky clothes to guard against the elements.

Drownproofing is a technique of floating that all boating enthusiasts should learn and master. It is particularly valuable, for it allows the person in the water to remain afloat for long periods of time with little or no energy expended. Moreover, it is a technique that can be quite successfully carried out even when fully clothed.

If you are not a reasonably good swimmer, you should never go out on a boat without wearing a life jacket. In addition, you should not attempt to learn this drownproofing technique unless you are a good swimmer, and under no circumstances should you attempt to learn it alone. Work with another competent swimmer, and practice by the side of a pool or close to the edge of a dock. Wear just a bathing suit at first. If you have any doubt about your swimming ability, seek professional help from a Red Cross or "Y" water-safety instructor.

Figure 113. The technique of "drownproofing." This life-saving procedure is possible because with few exceptions the body will float vertically when the lungs are fully inflated. See the text for details.

As Figure 113 shows, the floating or resting position, also called the front survival position, consists of the body being erect in the water, with the waist slightly flexed and the face tipped forward; the hands and arms dangle in a relaxed fashion. Hold your breath in this position for four or five seconds. At this point, in order to raise the head above water for a breath of air, use the arms and legs to propel the body upward, forcing the hands downward while doing a scissor kick. This lifts the body sufficiently for an inhalation. During the motion upward, while the face is still submerged, exhale fully through the nose. If this is done correctly, the head needs to be out of the water only long enough for an inhalation. After taking the fresh breath of air, tip your head forward again and allow the body to return to the original position. Rhythm is very important. Once you have mastered an easy, smooth cycle, you can float this way for very long periods of time indeed.

Mastering this skill will teach you a great deal about what type of clothing to wear while boating. As you practice with clothing on, you will discover that lightweight clothing that allows maximum movement is the best. We hope that you will never have to use this technique in seriousness. We hope also that should you find yourself in the water with a capsized boat, you will be able to stay with it and wait for help. On the other hand, the day may come when you are in the water separated from your boat. Your chances for survival will be much greater if you have made yourself "drownproof."

DISTRESS SIGNALS

Like it or not, every outboard skipper faces the prospect of an equipment breakdown someday. The problem may be a leaky fuel line, fouled plugs, or perhaps something as simple as running out of gas. In any event, the day will come when you will need help. In all probability, if you are in a small boat, you will have to rely on some means of communication other than a radio to summon help. Many boatmen think that all it takes is a shout or a wave of the arms to bring help. This just isn't so. Although most boating people stand ready to assist in an emergency (a tradition of the sea, by the way), they frequently misinterpret shouting and waving of the arms as friendly greetings and pass by without stopping.

Sometimes, when the victims of misfortune have no knowledge of the correct distress signals, it is purely a matter of luck that they obtain any

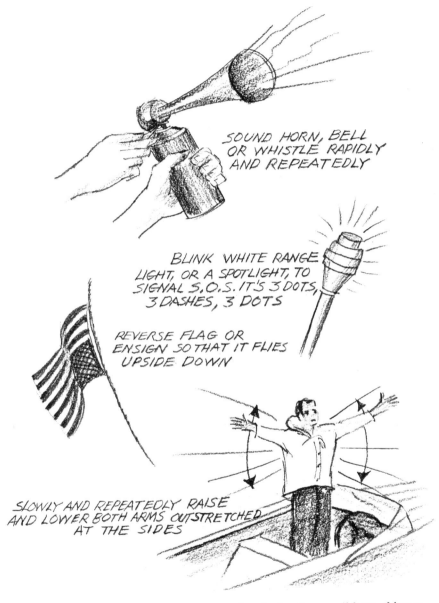

Figure 114. The most useful distress signals for the small-boat skipper. Never give a distress signal unless you mean it and are in need of assistance.

help at all. In one instance that I recall, three young boys in a fourteen-foot sailboat were anchored in a strong rip tide about two hundred yards offshore. The time was near nightfall. The boys were just sitting in the boat, caught in the grip of an apathy that was immediately noticeable. Evidently they had exhausted themselves shouting and waving at passing boats, and finally could do nothing but sit and wait for help. When they were finally approached by a boat under power, they explained that they had not been able to sail in against the rip tide, had become frightened, and then had anchored before trying to get help from a passing boat. But then, the people on every boat that went by simply waved back at them and continued on their way. If someone hadn't stopped to help, the boys would have been stranded after dark with no lights and no prospects for help.

There are several basic distress signals available to the small-boat skipper. These should be learned, and then used only in the event of distress. They should never be used in jest. Figure 114 shows what can be done. If you have no signaling equipment on board, stand up and slowly and repeatedly raise and lower both arms outstretched at the sides. This is a universally recognized distress signal and should bring help in quick order. If you have a horn or a whistle on board, try sounding it in repeated short blasts. At night, you can blink a flashlight in the time-honored S-O-S sequence; this is three short flashes, three long flashes, and three short flashes (- - -, —— ——, - - -). Finally, if you carry the ensign (the American flag) on board, you can fly it upside down to indicate that your boat is in distress.

COURTESY AFLOAT

All boatmen have equal rights and privileges when on the water. By the same token, however, all boatmen carry the responsibility to respect the rights of their fellows. This means much more than obeying the rules of the road to the letter. It involves anticipating the desires and movements of the other skipper's boat and then taking action to respect his rights.

In order to cover as many courtesy situations as possible, we will list them as a series of Do's and Don'ts. This will give you a quick reference for courtesy problems, and permit us to make the best use of available space.

Do stay clear of racing sailboats. If you must pass through a racing fleet, DO pass astern of all boats sailing closehauled, and DO keep to leeward of all boats running free.

Do go to the help of fellow boatmen in distress. This is a universal obligation. Always remember that tomorrow you may need help.

DON'T assume that, because you belong to a yacht club, all other clubs will automatically extend full privileges to you. When approaching a strange club for the first time, ask the attendant what privileges you are entitled to.

DON'T go aboard another boat until you are invited by the owner. It is considered a grave breach of etiquette to board a boat without an invitation.

Do be courteous and friendly to people in the unfamiliar harbors you visit. You will find that an outgoing, friendly manner will be received most cordially in most harbors.

Do anchor clear of channels and traffic lanes in strange anchorages. In addition, DON'T drop your anchor over another anchor line unless an emergency forces you to do so.

DON'T be a litterbug. Do save your garbage and trash in suitable containers until you can dispose of it ashore.

DON'T play a radio or phonograph late into the night in a crowded harbor. Many cruising boatmen go to bed with the sunset and get up with the sunrise.

DON'T butt in with unasked-for advice while aboard someone else's boat. Follow the wishes of the skipper while you are his guest. He expects to behave the same way aboard your boat.

DON'T abuse your right-of-way privilege over other boats. As pointed out earlier, it is often the better part of valor to give way in any situation that might endanger or otherwise inconvenience the other boat.

Do learn to recognize the skindiver's flag and stay clear of skindiving activities. The flag is bright red-orange with a diagonal white stripe.

DON'T tie up to government navigation buoys, or land at a private dock or float except in an emergency. The law forbids anyone to tie up at a navigation aid maintained or authorized by the Coast Guard, so think twice before tying up at a buoy, even in an emergency.

Do learn and obey the speed regulations for boats in channels and harbor areas, near bathing beaches, swimming platforms, etc.

Do operate at reduced speeds under conditions of reduced visibility.

DON'T ever operate a boat under the influence of intoxicating liquor or drugs.

14. GETTING THE MOST OUT OF YOUR BOAT

IT IS SAD TO RELATE, but many eager boat buyers wind up some months after their big purchase wondering what to do next with the boat. The first few times out they are caught up and thrilled by the speed, the excitement, and the exhilaration of being on the water. But then it all begins to seem old hat, like just another Sunday afternoon drive in the family car.

This is a very real problem, one that seems to hit owners of powerboats more often than sailing types. Sailors seem to revel in the interaction between wind, water, boat, crew, and skipper. For them, it is often quite enough to be in a responsive boat with a good breeze blowing. There is challenge enough in putting one's sailing skills to work; thus the sailor does not feel obligated to be under way to some predetermined point of destination.

All it takes to make a powerboat go is an engine, a throttle, and a steering wheel. There is obviously much more to powerboating, however, than punching the throttle and zooming out into open water. But for the skipper for whom this is all there is, boating may indeed become as dull as dishwater. With no place to go, and no constructive activity planned, this fellow might just as well give it up and go back to the Sunday drive.

Boating under power is like any other recreational activity. It will reward you in direct measure to what you put into it. Think of a boat as a great way to do nothing, and that's probably what you will do. Plan activities, involve your family and friends, and depart from the ordinary, however, and you should find boating most rewarding indeed.

Figure 115. The boat picnic is a great way for the family to get away from the hustle and bustle of everyday life. (*Photo courtesy of Johnson Motors.*)

WHERE THE ACTION IS

Any attempt to cover all the fun activities available to powerboat owners will of necessity be incomplete, for each boating locality will have its own unique activities and each ingenious skipper will invent uses for his boat that give him and his friends special satisfactions. What follows, therefore, is but a survey—an introduction to the many different leisure activities available to the outboard owner.

Picnicking. If you are a victim of the urban madhouse, or if you just want some peace and quiet with your family or friends, plan a boating picnic. Lightweight portable ice chests and beverage coolers are now available in a variety of sizes and price ranges. To avoid messy clean-up chores, instead of ice use the bagged coolants that are frozen in the home freezer prior to placing them in the ice chest. Plan your menu to suit your own needs, but avoid the temptation to take too much food and drink. Just about the only drawback to a boat picnic is the weight of the gear you'll be taking aboard, and of course how far you will have to

Figure 116. Whether on a pontoon boat, cruiser, or even a runabout, entertaining afloat is a fine way to enjoy the company of your friends. (*Photo courtesy of Kiekhaefer Mercury.*)

Figure 117. The boat camper uses his boat to carry the camping gear to a favored spot, and then enjoys the many pleasures of camping and boating alike. (*Photo courtesy of Kiekhaefer Mercury.*)

carry it. It's all well worth the effort, however, as you will discover when you have found an isolated beach, a remote little island, or perhaps a secluded cove complete with cooling breezes, privacy, and no ants.

Entertaining afloat. Many boat owners overlook a marvelous opportunity to entertain their friends on the often mistaken assumption that people who don't own boats do not like being on the water. There are people, to be sure, who would rather do anything than set foot on a boat. Such landlubbers, fortunately, are in the minority. Most people, if given the chance, are quite excited about spending some time on the water. Give some thought, however, to the desires and experience of your prospective guests, and plan your outing accordingly. A fast run in deep water with heavy pounding and flying spray will please some, but frighten the wits out of others. For the more inexperienced or timid, content yourself with low-speed excursions in quiet and sheltered waters until your guests request more action.

Boat camping. Even though your boat is not equipped with sleeping facilities, a galley, and a head, do not rule out overnight trips as a worthwhile activity. It doesn't take a very large boat to store and carry

Figure 118. Boat camping in reverse. This savvy family trailers a boat along with their camp trailer, thus opening up new avenues for outdoor fun. (*Photo courtesy of Kiekhaefer Mercury.*)

the needed gear for camping ashore: a collapsible tent, sleeping bags, cooking gear, ice chest, cooler, and perhaps one of the newer portable self-contained toilets. Adding this overnight capability brings other dividends. It more than doubles your weekend cruising range, for example, in addition to bringing previously unattainable ports within reach. Moreover, just as many boat campers today carry their camping gear aboard boats, we are seeing more and more trailer campers trailering boats as well. This might be called boat camping in reverse. The benefits are obvious both in terms of the variety of waterways available for exploration and in terms of expanded activities while camped.

Cruising or boat camping in a group. Cruising is a way of life for many boating people. Outboarders, too, enjoy this rewarding mode of recreational travel when they own properly equipped craft. Perhaps it is the complete change of pace that makes cruising such a satisfying pastime.

Figure 119. Many young couples, as well as others, are discovering the joys of cruising aboard fast and economical-to-run craft such as this one. With a couple of berths, a head, and perhaps a small galley, the necessities are met while cruising from port to port. (*Photo courtesy of Johnson Motors.*)

Figure 120. The gunkholer finds reward enough in exploring strange inlets, bays, and other out-of-the-way places. Occasionally, however, a treasure such as this old anchor turns up. (*Photo courtesy of Kiekhaefer Mercury.*)

More than one cruising skipper, caught in the daily nine-to-five routine of commuting and work the rest of the year, has been heard to exclaim over the joys of leisurely cruising from port to port and of turning in at sundown and rising at sunup. Cruising in the generally accepted sense, however, is available only to those whose craft are adequately equipped. For the rest, boat camping is the best that can be managed. For boat campers and cruising skippers 'alike, however, there is a way to heighten the pleasures of traveling on the water. Go as part of a group. There's much to be said for the common joy of breaking camp or weighing anchor and heading out as a group for the next port of call. Evenings, too, are more enjoyable as people gather on boats rafted together or around a campfire to share the experiences of the day. Many boating or yacht clubs and local U. S. Power Squadrons conduct group cruises for their members. These are often most memorable events.

Gunkholing. For the naturally curious skipper, very few boating activities surpass gunkholing. This is simply the art of searching out and exploring out-of-the-way places. The gunkholer is in his glory when poking up a hidden stream, into a secluded bay, or along a desolate reach of white sandy beach. The rewards are usually the peace and quiet of an isolated place; sometimes, however, an interesting remnant of another age is discovered. Regardless of what is found, however, gunkholing is always an adventure for the curious at heart.

Diving. As exciting as the surface of the water can be, it's nothing compared to the beauty and mystery of the underwater world—assuming, of course, that the water is clear. Today's would-be diver has but two choices; he can use scuba (self-contained underwater breathing apparatus) gear, or he can slip on a mask and fins and hold his breath while underwater. The diver who holds his breath is limited to about one to two minutes underwater. The scuba diver, on the other hand, has a forty-to-fifty-minute air supply. This is often more than enough time to make diving well worth the effort. Scuba divers find a great deal of pleasure in spear fishing, underwater photography, shell collecting, treasure hunting, cave diving, wreck exploring, or simply poking about underwater. For those interested in this sport, there are three basic requirements for maximum safety. (1) All divers should be strong swimmers, and should have previous open-water diving experience. (2) All divers should be physically and psychologically fit. (3) No one should dive until he has completed a course taught by a certified scuba

Figure 121. When properly trained and equipped, the scuba diver finds the undersea world a rich and fascinating place. (*Photo courtesy of Marine Products Operations, Chrysler Corporation.*)

instructor. Such courses are often sponsored or given by dive shops; your local "Y" may offer a course also. When you are actually diving, there are two additional rules that must be followed: *Never dive alone!* and *Always fly the "diver down" flag!* This flag is bright red-orange with a white stripe running diagonally from the staff corner to the opposite corner. Fly the flag at least three feet above the highest point of the boat.

If the water is exceptionally clear, *snorkeling* is another way to enjoy the beauty of the underwater world. The snorkel is a J-shaped tube with a mouthpiece at the end of the curve at the base. When snorkeling, you swim face down at the surface or just below the surface with the long end of the snorkel tube projecting into the air. With the unlimited supply of air this technique provides, it is possible to paddle about and view the bottom for hours on end.

Figure 122. Water skiing is an exciting and demanding sport. Note the safety precautions in use here: The skier is wearing a flotation belt, there is an observer in the boat, and the skiing is on open water away from other craft. (*Photo courtesy of Kiekhaefer Mercury.*)

Water skiing. You'll find water skiers on any body of smooth water large enough to accommodate them. There's a good reason for this. Water skiing is just about the fastest and most exciting water sport available, short of high-speed racing. It is a skill that almost everyone can master,

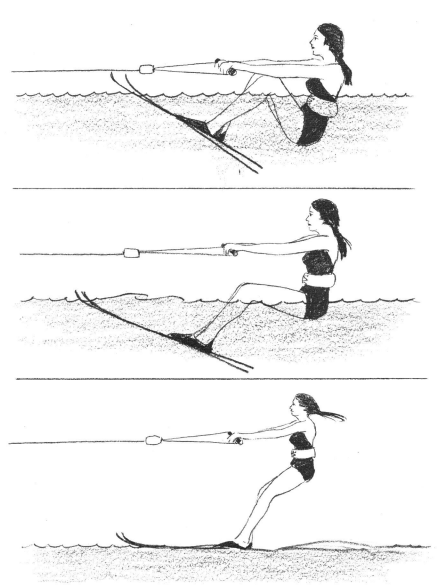

Figure 123. How to get up on water skis. See the text for details.

and it does not require a large outlay of money to get started. All that is needed, in addition to a boat that will do eighteen to twenty miles per hour when towing, is a set of skis, a tow line with a handle, and a flotation belt. For maximum safety, there should always be an observer in the boat in addition to the boat's operator. Getting up on skis seems difficult at first. A bit of practice, however, usually does the trick. As Figure 123

Figure 124. To signal your wishes to the tow boat when water skiing, learn these standard hand and arm signals.

shows, the best way to start is to sit on the back of the skis, with their tips above the surface of the water in front of you. When you are in position, shout "Hit it!" to the boat operator. Then, as the boat accelerates and as you rise, keep your legs bent and your arms straight. Let the boat pull you—don't lean forward. Before you know it, you'll be skimming along with the best of them. Signaling your wishes to the boat

Figure 125. This fast and easy-to-handle inflatable outboard is the ideal craft for a father-and-son fishing trip. (*Photo courtesy of Avon Rubber Co., Ltd.*)

might be a problem, if it weren't for a set of hand and arm signals worked out by the American Water Ski Association. These are shown in Figure 124. One final word about water skiing: If you don't want to wear out your welcome and otherwise antagonize fellow boatmen, do your water skiing on open water, not near and around anchored and moored boats. There are very few things more annoying to the people aboard an anchored boat than the noise, spray, and water turbulence produced by reckless or thoughtless water skiers.

Fishing and hunting. There is obviously no need to belabor this most popular of boating activities. Few indeed are the men and boys who do not know or look forward to the joys of a fishing trip. From the youngster dropping his first dough-baited bent-pin hook into a quiet pond to the master deep-sea fisherman angling for marlin or tuna, the potential for fishing of a well-equipped outboard is perfectly clear. Owners and renters alike by the thousands pursue this inexpensive and interesting sport. Duck hunters, too, often the same people who some weeks earlier were happy fishing from their craft, find an outboard the ideal means

Figure 126. Depending on his choice of boat and engine, the outboard skipper can try his luck on a quiet lake or stream or even go offshore after the big ones. (*Photo courtesy of Aquasport, Inc.*)

Figure 127. Don't put the boat up just because summer is over. It's often the best (if not only) way to get to the shooting grounds. (*Photo courtesy of Kiekhaefer Mercury.*)

of getting to the hunting grounds. If you want to know more about using your boat for either fishing or hunting, you will find numerous sources of information right in your own community. Clubs, sporting goods and tackle stores, boat dealers, boat liveries, bait shops, and even your neighbors all can help.

Competition. For those interested in pitting their skills against others, there are at least two popular forms of competition available to the powerboat skipper: *predicted logging* and *racing*. The predicted logger uses his knowledge of his boat, the wind, and the prevailing currents to predict how long it will take him to cruise between several predetermined points. The hitch is that he runs the courses without a speedometer or watch. In predicted-log races the competition is both against one's own navigation and seamanship ability and the other competitors entered in the event. The skipper who comes closest to his predicted time is the winner. One might ask, however, how close a skipper has to come to satisfy himself. Predicted logging is an activity that greatly sharpens a skipper's ability to navigate his boat.

There's a potential race whenever two impatient skippers with powerful rigs encounter each other. Impromptu racing can be great fun, if there is no threat of wash, noise, or even collision to other people using the waterway. Better yet is class racing. This activity is well organized and is available to anyone interested in and willing to abide by the rules.

TRAILERING

One of the great advantages of owning a small boat is that it need not be moored in a permanent anchorage or berthed in a slip. Instead, it can be stored anywhere you like on a trailer. Another advantage is that virtually all bodies of water that have launching ramps are available for boating fun. Small boats kept in the water, on the other hand, are confined to the immediate area of home port.

Selecting a trailer for a boat requires careful thought. The trailer should provide support in the right places, so that the hull will not sag and lose its shape. With respect to the size of the trailer, follow this rule of thumb: Take the total weight of the boat fully equipped; if this figure is within one hundred pounds of the rated capacity of a trailer, choose the next larger trailer.

A well-designed trailer will meet all local and state regulations and will provide good riding comfort with maximum safety in the towing car. Of great importance, dry launching with a minimum of physical effort should be possible. If you are in doubt, consult a dealer who is familiar with the different types of trailers and what they are designed to do. Buying a trailer is somewhat like buying tires; safety and reliability depend on quality.

Load distribution is an important factor in how well a boat on a trailer will ride. In general, the boat's center of gravity should be a bit forward of the trailer wheels. This will produce sufficient weight at the tongue of the trailer—something in excess of one hundred pounds. Take care to adjust this bumperweight figure. If tongue weight is too great, the rear of the car will be forced down. If it is too little, the trailer will bob up and down at the rear bumper and produce a very uneven and unsafe ride. It's quite simple to shift the center of gravity of a boat on a trailer. Simply move the contents of the boat forward or aft to obtain a better balance.

A number of special precautionary measures when you are driving are necessary with a trailer following behind. First, check the trailer regulations to make sure your rig complies with those of all the states within which you plan to travel. For example, you will probably need a rear light that includes a brake signal and directional signals, and you may need brakes on the trailer itself. Launch only at approved hard-surfaced ramps to avoid getting your trailer and car stuck in sand or mud. When you are on the road, remember that you are carrying an extra-heavy load and that a much greater stopping distance is required. Also remember to swing wide when passing and to allow extra room up ahead.

Most drivers experience their greatest difficulty when they are backing a trailer. Some practice in an open area such as a parking lot is needed, of course, but if you remember to turn the steering wheel opposite to the direction in which you want the rear of the trailer to turn, you should minimize this difficulty. For example, to turn the rear of the trailer to the left, turn the steering wheel to the right. Try it, but practice in a light-traffic area before attempting to launch a boat. A simpler rule of thumb to follow in backing a trailer is to place your hand at the *bottom* of the steering wheel. With your steering hand in this position, to back the trailer to the *left* you move your hand and the bottom of the wheel to the *left.* Conversely, when you move your hand to the *right* the trailer will go right.

Figure 128. A camper on wheels and a trailered boat make an ideal combination for roaming far and wide at reasonable cost. (*Photo courtesy of Marine Products Operations, Chrysler Corporation.*)

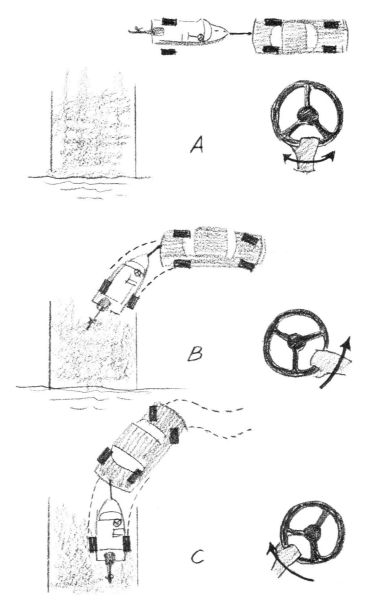

Figure 129. How to back a trailer and boat down a ramp to the water. See the text for details.

To get a better picture of how this works, let's imagine we are about to launch a boat. In Figure 129(A) the boat and trailer are being backed into position prior to turning onto the ramp. It's impossible to steer a straight path when you are backing a trailer, so don't try. Move your hand and the wheel back and forth over short intervals to maintain as straight a path as possible. When the boat is in position to turn down the ramp, shift your hand and the bottom of the wheel to the right, and the trailer will turn in the same direction onto the ramp [Figure 129 (B)]. To make the trailer turn left—that is, to straighten it on the ramp (and keep it from running right off the ramp while it is swinging to the right)—move your hand and the bottom of the wheel to the left. The trailer will then shift to the left and in effect straighten up as it moves down the ramp [Figure 129(C)].

Launching a boat from a trailer is a bit more complex than it might appear at first glance. This is so, largely, because there are numerous small tasks that must be accomplished in conjunction with the major task—getting the boat into the water and under way. Starting in the parking area, before backing the trailer onto the ramp, you should free the boat of all tie downs *except* the winch cable, install the drain plug, stow all gear needed for the outing, and make paddles, a boat hook, and the necessary lines ready for use. In addition, if removable, the trailer tail-light assembly should be removed and the trailer wiring plug should be disconnected from the car.

When you have accomplished these preliminary steps, the boat and trailer wheels are just about at the water's edge. At this point a member of your crew should go aboard the boat and lower the engine into the drive position. Now back the trailer down the ramp until the lower unit of the engine is deep enough in the water to pick up cooling water. Have your crew member start the engine and warm it up for a few minutes. You'll know the engine is warmed up if it does not stall when shifted into *reverse*. If possible, have someone stand to one side of the ramp and hold a long bow line to prevent the boat from floating away should the engine stall.

At this point disconnect the winch hook from the bow eye and then back the trailer down until the stern of the boat floats free. It may be necessary to shove the boat to free it from the trailer. Take care, however, not to back up too far; there's nothing more humiliating (and infuriating to others waiting for the ramp) than a tow car stalled and half sunk at the end of a launching ramp.

With the boat afloat and under its own power, haul out the trailer and park it. The rest of the party can then be taken aboard off the beach or at a nearby dock or float.

In essence, getting the boat back on the trailer is just the reverse of launching. This maneuver may or may not be easier than launching. It all depends on your equipment and of course on the skill you display in using it. In general, however, you begin the recovery procedure exactly where the launching procedure ended—with the trailer in position at the end of the ramp. It may be necessary to run the trailer a bit deeper into the water to get the boat in position and started onto the trailer. Be sure the trailer is at right angles to the water's edge. This helps in lining up the boat. If your seamanship skill permits it, use the engine (at idling speeds only) to nudge the boat into position at the rear of the trailer. Approach slowly and allow for current and wind drift. If you are apprehensive about using the engine—don't. Paddle in instead. In either case, however, put out a bow line to a man on shore, and use his muscle to help start the boat onto the trailer. Once the boat is started and lined up properly, fasten the winch cable and draw it up taut. Then have your crew get out of the boat before winching in to avoid unnecessary strain on the winch. Pull the drain plug before leaving to drain any water taken aboard.

The final step is to get the boat and trailer off the ramp and then prepare it for the road. The tie downs should be fastened and all gear secured as it was for the trip to the water.

Trailering offers the outboard skipper unlimited boating horizons. It would be unfair, however, to imply that maneuvering a trailer is a simple and totally uncomplicated affair. Quite the opposite is the case. The rewards of trailering, however, far outweigh the learning and practice needed for efficiency. For thousands who have tried it, it is the only way to go!

15.   CARING FOR YOUR BOAT

ALTHOUGH THIS IS THE LAST CHAPTER of *The Complete Beginner's Guide to Outboarding,* it is by no means the least important. Just as the sheer fun of boating is partially counterbalanced by the inevitable element of danger, the enjoyment of well-maintained equipment is offset by the need for year-round maintenance. There is no escaping it. The elements and hard use combine to take a heavy toll on paint, varnish, gel coat, engine, and trailer unless continual efforts are made to keep an outfit in top shape.

There are two aspects to caring for your boat. One has to do with where you will keep it. Many small-boat owners trailer their boats, while others use the facilities of a yacht club, marina, or boatyard. We have already discussed trailering in some detail. The other aspect of caring for your rig has to do with maintenance. As you will discover, this is a year-round chore. There is no need, however, to look at maintenance with any sense of foreboding. When the necessary upkeep chores on a boat and trailer are performed in a routine manner the year round, these responsibilities become a natural but not burdensome part of boating. Of course, if your boat is an old "clunker," you may find maintenance occupying all your time and effort, to the exclusion of any fun on the water.

As pointed out earlier, modern methods of construction using the most up-to-date materials have given us durable and relatively easy-to-maintain hulls, engines, and trailers. Hulls of Fiberglas and aluminum, corrosion-resistant alloys in engines, galvanized steel in trailers, and waterproof grease in trailer wheels all help to reduce maintenance chores. Synthetic lines have replaced Manila lines, also helping to reduce the cost of operating a boat. Finally, modern antifouling paints keep a boat's bottom relatively clean compared to what the boat owner faced just a few years ago.

YACHT CLUB, MARINA, OR BOATYARD?

The boat owner has a choice of summer accommodations for his boat. He may elect a trailer for his craft and store the boat in the backyard between outings. This is one of the least expensive ways to enjoy boating, but it does involve learning to handle a trailer rig. Other choices include a yacht club, a marina, or a boatyard. Whichever you choose, however, there are just a few ways to tie up and store a boat. The most convenient, and often the most expensive, is the *floating dock*. This rides up and down with the tide and provides a narrow dock next to the boat from which it is boarded quite easily. A less expensive choice is a *slip* between pilings. A boat in a slip rides up and down with the tide, requiring that care be taken when docking lines are put out, for the pilings and any walks constructed on them are immovable. As a result, tying up and getting on and off a boat may be difficult at low tide.

For the majority of boat owners, the *offshore mooring* seems to be the most attractive way to keep a boat in the water. A sound mooring, which should be designed for local conditions, is lower in cost than a trailer. To determine what is the best mooring rig for local conditions, consult the harbor master, dock master of the yacht club, or proprietor of the marina or boatyard. In many localities you may simply choose an open spot and put down your mooring. If you do this, of course, maintenance of the mooring is your responsibility. You will need to make arrangements to put the mooring in at the beginning of the season and take it out at the end of the season. Moorings maintained by yacht clubs, marinas, or boatyards, and sometimes by coastal towns, however, are rented out by the season. These range in cost from the very modestly priced town moorings to the very expensive yacht club and marina moorings with launch and other special services.

There isn't room here to describe in detail the different services offered by yacht clubs, marinas, and boatyards. We can, however, give you a brief description of the various services and encourage you to investigate

Figure 130. Education begins early in this trailer-boat family. With a litterbag aboard, this youngster will learn not to dump refuse into our already threatened waterways. (*Photo courtesy of Evinrude Motors.*)

thoroughly before you make a decision. Boating pleasure depends upon a happy frame of mind. If you are dissatisfied in any way with the service you are receiving from your club, marina, or boatyard, the chances are that the hours spent aboard your boat will be somewhat less than completely gratifying.

Yacht clubs range in size and services from the small club devoted exclusively to sailing activities, to large and elaborate organizations for the owners of all types of boats that offer year-round social and recreational activities. In some of these larger organizations, the social and recreational activities have grown to the point that boating has become a secondary activity. There is probably no such thing as the typical yacht club. If one did exist, however, it would probably offer instruction in sailing, small-boat handling, seamanship, swimming, and safety. It would also conduct a full summer calendar of races and cruises and perhaps two or three major summer social affairs.

The marina is a relatively new development in boating services. In many ways, the marina is a cross between the yacht club and boatyard.

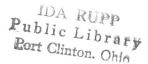

It offers those services of both that are in greatest demand by the boating public. It might be said that the marina is a commercial yacht club. Services that can be expected are a mooring or a slip; a clean and well-laid-out dock and parking area; a gasoline dock; some repair and maintenance services, including outdoor winter storage; the capacity to launch and take out fairly large boats; a clubhouse-type building often containing a snack bar, toilet and shower facilities, a marine stores shop, lockers, and other facilities; and finally, attendants and watchmen to police the entire area. Some marinas are excellent, but others are little more than boating slums. Thus care is required when a marina is selected.

The boatyard represents the most primitive commercially run home for your boat. You can expect crude docking and mooring facilities, lockers in some but not all boatyards, and occasionally toilet and shower facilities. Boatyards generally do not offer launch service, but there may be one or two old rowboats available for getting out to moored boats. A plus for boatyards is repair and maintenance service. This is the real reason for the boatyard's existence, so you can expect these services to be good. Many boatyards rent space for winter storage and will permit a certain amount of do-it-yourself work on a boat. Many marinas also permit do-it-yourself activities, but both usually require that you purchase tools and supplies through the yard and not elsewhere. In addition, you will probably not be permitted to bring in outside labor to work on your boat.

SPRING CARE

After the long winter storage period, either indoors or outside, a boat requires certain work before it can be launched for the new season. If you have performed all the necessary fall lay-up chores conscientiously, getting your boat back on the water is an invigorating and satisfying activity. If you neglected those fall tasks, however, you will probably be late getting back on the water and lose a lot of boating enjoyment.

If the boat is to remain in the water all season long, it will be necessary to coat the bottom with antifouling paint. There are several different types of antifouling paint, as well as different formulas for salt and fresh water. The best procedure is to inquire about the most effective type of paint for your area. As you will discover, some paints seem to perform better than others. Of course, if you plan to trailer your boat, antifouling paint is not necessary, for the boat will probably not be in the water long enough for any bottom growth to develop. There isn't room here to discuss in detail other painting tasks you may face. The hull or topside of the boat, for example, may require painting. If this is the case, it would be wise to consult a local marine-paint dealer for the best paint available.

Another necessary spring chore is varnishing the *brightwork*. You will discover that much of the varnished woodwork on the boat will need a new coat or two every year. Sand the old coat down with fine sandpaper before applying the new coat. If the old varnish is checked or otherwise broken, consult the instructions on the varnish can for preparing the surface.

Getting your engine ready for use following winter storage has been discussed elsewhere. Follow those recommendations or the instructions provided by the engine manufacturer. In addition, clean all metal parts and polish them to protect against the elements. Make a particularly close inspection of the steering assembly. Look for excessive wear, and check to be sure that the pulleys are free and that the cables are not excessively corroded. Thoroughly clean the interior of the boat, and return all loose gear that you removed at fall lay-up time. Finally, run through a checklist of required and extra safety gear, and repair or replace wherever necessary.

If your boat has exposed aluminum parts, it will be necessary to clean them with an abrasive substance and then apply polish or wax. Aluminum oxidizes, and over the winter it will collect a layer of oxide scale. Anodized aluminum, on the other hand, does not need to be scrubbed down with an abrasive. It only requires a good washing before application of a protective coating of wax. A good-quality automobile wax does a very satisfactory job.

MIDSEASON CARE

Care for your boat does not end once it has been launched. Throughout the boating season, there are a number of inspection and maintenance chores you should carry out routinely. All lines, for example, should be inspected for wear each time you go out. In addition, make periodic checks of the steering assembly and follow the procedures discussed earlier with respect to the engine. If you are going to keep your boat in the water, and perhaps race it, its bottom will need periodic cleaning. This is especially true if the boat is to be left in the water all season long. Even the best antifouling paints will not prevent the growth of marine or aquatic slimes. As a result, it will be necessary to haul the boat out for a good scrub every month or six weeks. Another way to do it is to bring the boat in close to shore and then go into the water to scrub down the bottom. This takes a good swimmer, for it is necessary to take a deep breath and duck under while scrubbing. I remember doing this as a youngster in Maine waters. Believe me, we scrubbed all the harder because the water was so cold!

If you think of your boat as a structure that requires maintaining, it becomes easier to attend to the routine inspections needed to keep it in top condition. Actually, little more than a watchful eye is required, followed up immediately with service or repair, to keep your boat in top condition. But it is necessary to "think maintenance," for a boat will go downhill rapidly if it is not cared for. This is part of the fun of boating, however. A skipper takes pride in his craft; thus he willingly assumes responsibility for its condition.

The owner of a trailer must also attend to certain maintenance chores. A trailer, after all, is a mechanical device. As such, it is subject to the wear and deterioration that befall all of man's mechanical inventions. With the unique exposure a trailer receives—periodic dunking of the wheels, repeated wettings, and prolonged periods out in the elements—the key to maintenance is prevention of potential problems. This means anticipating what might happen by taking preventive steps.

Consider the wheels first, since they are the most important part of your trailer. Whether it is brand-new or used, the first thing you should do with a trailer is check the wheel bearings to see that they are properly packed. Too often for comfort, wheel bearings are ignored, and a potentially pleasant boating trip comes a cropper.

Investigate the use of waterproof bearing caps, and have them installed if it is possible to do so. In any event, be sure to use waterproof trailer bearing grease; a dealer will tell you where to get it if you plan to service the trailer yourself.

With repeated submersion of the wheels during the boating season, periodic inspection of wheel bearings is a must. If your trailer uses full-size wheels and tires, plan to inspect the bearings at two-thousand-mile intervals. If waterproof bearing caps and waterproof grease are used, the

Figure 131. Midseason care includes preventive maintenance on the propeller shaft. Follow the recommendations given in Chapter 5. (*Photo courtesy of Johnson Motors.*)

bearings should go up to ten thousand miles on a pack. The effects of submersion are insidious, however, and it isn't safe to count on more than about two thousand miles. The smaller tires and wheels, on the other hand, must rotate about twice as many times as standard wheels for a given distance. These wheels must therefore be inspected more often—at seven-hundred-to-eight-hundred-mile intervals is about right.

Brakes are almost as important as wheel bearings. If your trailer has brakes, follow the recommended maintenance procedures faithfully. Moreover, unless you are a skilled mechanic, it is wiser to have the brakes serviced by a dealer.

Other points on a trailer that usually need lubrication are grease fittings on spring mounts, the bow winch, the tongue dolly wheel, and hull roller wheels (if your trailer has them). Inspect these moving parts before each trip and keep them oiled and free.

Trailer boatmen who launch and recover their boats from seawater face a special problem. Salty seawater is particularly corrosive to metal parts, and must be rinsed away after each exposure. Hose down the entire trailer (and boat, too) with fresh water after exposure to seawater. And don't make the mistake of assuming that corrosion stops after the seawater has dried. This is simply not true; the corrosive action of the salt crystals continues even after the water has evaporated.

Because the average boat buyer has just so many dollars to invest, there is a tendency to purchase something less than top quality in a trailer in order to get the best boat possible. If this is the case with your rig, it should be obvious that careful trailer maintenance is a must. What good are the most elaborate plans and a great boat if the trailer won't take you to the water?

FALL CARE

Fall means the end of the boating season for most boatmen. Of course, those who live in states such as Florida and California can enjoy boating all year round. These folk are to be envied by the rest of us who must lay up our boats for the long winter. Preparing a boat for winter storage consists of much more than just hauling it out and throwing a tarpaulin over the top. Certain chores must be performed if the boat is to get through the winter without damage, and if getting it back into the water the following spring is to be accomplished easily.

The first task following hauling is to scrub the bottom. This is most easily done immediately upon hauling, not the next day or some other later time. The growth that has accumulated on the bottom comes off most easily while still wet. Once it has had a chance to dry out, removal is extremely difficult. Many yards include scrubbing the bottom in the price of hauling the boat and setting it in its cradle for winter storage. This is all well and good, but you should go over the bottom yourself to make sure it is thoroughly clean. Very often areas of the hull are overlooked, and if the boat was taken out by means of a travel lift, the portions of the hull under the lifting straps were probably not scrubbed down.

After the boat has been placed in its cradle or trailer, check to be sure that the hull is supported at all the proper spots. A hull out of the water is subject to many weight strains it does not experience in the water. While in the water, the hull is supported by water pressure at every point below the waterline. Too often hulls sag and seams part because boats were put up for winter storage quickly and carelessly.

All loose gear should be removed from the boat before putting on the winter cover. Be especially careful to remove items that may be affected by cold weather. Above all, do not leave any food aboard. It will just attract insects and mice, and also confront you with a messy situation when you pull off the winter cover the following spring.

Fall is the time to make an extra effort when putting the boat up for storage, for everything that is not done then must be done the following spring. Given the eagerness to get back on the water all boatmen feel in the spring, doesn't it make sense to do as much as possible when laying the boat up at the end of the season? We think it does, and having experienced both situations, we can attest to the joy and pleasure of getting the boat back into the water with the least fuss and bother at the beginning of the boating season.

INDEX

INDEX

lift, 24, 26–28
thrust, 24, 26–28
weight, 24, 26–28
Forward spring line, 106
Fronts, types of, 124–27
 cold, 124, 126–27
 occluded, 124, 126
 stationary, 124, 126
 warm, 124, 126
Fueling safety, 68–70
Fuel system, 52

G

Gale warning, 128–31
Government publications, 153
Ground tackle, 112
Gunkholing, 210–11

H

Handling characteristics of outboards, 88–90
Heavy seas
 handling a boat in, 140–43
Heavy weather boating, 134–45
High pressure systems, 122–23
Hitches, 76–77
Horsepower and boat size, 50–51
Houseboat, 16–17
Hull construction materials, 28–32
Hull types, 19–25
 arc-bottom, 22, 25
 deep-V bottom, 22–23, 25
 displacement, 19–22, 24
 flat-bottom, 22, 25
 planing, 19–22, 24–28
 round-bottom, 22, 24
 V-bottom, 22, 25
Hunting, 216, 218
Hurricane, 121–22
 warning, 128, 131

I

Ignition system, 52

K

Knot (nautical mile), 168
Knots, 74–75

L

Land breeze, 123–25
Lapstrake hull, 29
Latitude, 179, 180–81
Launching from a trailer, 223
Lead line, 161
Leaving a dock, 85–87
Life Preserver (personal flotation device), 186–88
Line of position, 178
Loading a trailer from water, 224
Locks, 110
Long splice, 79
Longitude, 179, 180–81
LOP, 178
Lower unit, 52
Low pressure systems, 122–23

M

"Magic circle," 173
Magnetic bearings, 166
Man overboard, 197–98
"Mare's tail" clouds, 126, 129
Marina, characteristics of, 227–28
Marlinspike seamanship, 73–82
Mental dead reckoning, 184
Midseason care, 229–32
Molded-plywood hull, 30
Motorboat, definition of, 2
Motorboats, classification of, 2–3
Mushroom anchor, 112–13